D1651119

CHINESE POEMS IN
ENGLISH RHYME

THE UNIVERSITY OF CHICAGO PRESS
CHICAGO, ILLINOIS

• • •

THE BAKER & TAYLOR COMPANY
NEW YORK

THE CAMBRIDGE UNIVERSITY PRESS
LONDON

THE MARUZEN-KABUSHIKI-KAISHA
TOKYO, OSAKA, KYOTO, FUKUOKA, SENDAI

THE COMMERCIAL PRESS, LIMITED
SHANGHAI

CHINESE POEMS IN ENGLISH RHYME

唐詩英韻

By ADMIRAL TS'AI T'ING-KAN

蔡 廷 幹

AUTHOR OF A SYNTHETIC STUDY OF LAO
TZŬ'S TAO-TÊ-CHING IN CHINESE

老 解 老

THE UNIVERSITY OF CHICAGO PRESS
CHICAGO · ILLINOIS

PL
2956
T87C
COPY 2

COPYRIGHT 1932 BY THE UNIVERSITY OF CHICAGO
ALL RIGHTS RESERVED. PUBLISHED SEPTEMBER 1932
· · ·
COMPOSED AND PRINTED BY THE UNIVERSITY OF CHICAGO
PRESS, CHICAGO, ILLINOIS, U.S.A.

TO THE MEMORY OF
MY FATHER AND MOTHER

FOREWORD

It is an unusual honor to be allowed to write a few lines to announce the splendid work which Admiral Ts'ai has done in translating into English one hundred and twenty-two selected poems of the T'ang period. For fifteen years he worked steadily, taking great pains to secure the right rendering of each line and each phrase. As a result he has succeeded in presenting to the world a small volume which is almost an exact reproduction in English of the Chinese. To preserve the spirit and music of the original and to attain a natural flow of language in the translation is a rare combination of achievements. None but an artist could do it.

If we mistake not, this volume is the first English translation of Chinese poems by a native of China. There have been several translations by foreigners, among whom one remembers Miss Amy Lowell especially. But to Admiral Ts'ai goes the distinction of being the first Chinese to work in English verse. This is the more remarkable when one recalls that usually his name is not associated with the literary profession. One would rather expect from him a treatise on political science or some phase of government. And, as a matter of fact, a man who is a practical statesman cannot conceal himself, hard as he may try. His selection of poems betrays him. He could not escape the influence of his professional interest. These verses will be found to present a philosophical

·vii·

view of China's political ideals. For this reason, even students of politics should find this volume interesting.

With these brief words it is a great pleasure to present to the public Admiral Ts'ai's poems, which are sure to make a distinct contribution to the cause of international understanding.

L. T. CHEN, *Executive Secretary*
China Council
Institute of Pacific Relations

July 5, 1930

PREFACE

These translations of Chinese poetry into English verse were begun thirty years ago. The originals are found in the first and third books of the 千家詩 *Ch'ien Chia Shih*, "Selected Poems from Many Poets." Each poem is composed of four lines of either five or seven words to each line.

In translating these poems the rule followed was that each Chinese word be equal to one foot or two syllables in English. Thus, in poems of five Chinese words in each line the pentameter was used. In poems of seven words in the line, the hexameter was generally used. There are a few exceptions to the foregoing rules.

The prevailing meter is iambic. Elisions have been avoided as far as possible so as not to mar the words, giving the readers the credit of knowing how to treat the words to suit the rhythm in the scanning and reading of the translations. An exception exists in poem No. 119 where the word occurs twice. In the third line "flow'rs" has an elision, making it one syllable to fit into the rhythm of the verse, while for the same reason "flowers" in the fourth line is unaltered, retaining its two syllables. Where this word occurs only once in any poem it may be treated as either of one or two syllables. The word "balcony" in poem No. 88 is considered a word of two syllables and "many," wherever it occurs, is treated as a word of one syllable. A few elisions were unavoidable.

A friend has pointed out that in some lines the ictus is thrown

·ix·

on unimportant and unemphatic words, such as "it," "of," etc. This may appear to weaken the construction of the verse but it is found in the best of English poetry, even in such a purist as Pope. The stress may fall on such words in scanning but in reading they may not be emphasized. There is rather an advantage in tripping lightly over them, since it gives life and airiness to the verse.

I have not followed the Chinese order of rhyme which generally begins in the first line, followed by the second and fourth, or begins in the second and followed by the fourth. The forms I have employed are the rhyming couplets and alternate rhymes to avoid the frequent repetition of the same sound which may tire the ear. The rhymes are masculine and are perfect as far as I am aware. The rhymes in these translations grow out of the words expressed or out of the sense implied. For instance, in the third line of poem No. 77, "set" is implied or understood by the morning moon having been so low down as to be in a line with the house and trees, while "yet," the rhyming word, is expressed by the Chinese words 未曾 *wei ts'êng*, "not yet," the exact English equivalent. In poem No. 100, "bare" in the first line is the translation for 空 *k'ung*, "empty," "bare," while the rhyming word, "air," in the second line is the translation for 風 *feng*, "wind," "air," etc. "Fled" in the third line is the translation for 無覓處 *wu mi ch'u*, "nowhere to be found"—fled, flown, gone. "Spread" in the fourth line, the rhyming word for "fled," is meant to express 滿 *man*, "full," "filled to overflow," or "thickly spread" as I put it. It was not intended that the sense of the original should be warped and twisted to suit the exigency of rhyme.

Instead of writing a long and tedious preface to explain the technique of Chinese poetry it is my intention to write a companion volume to this work to explain in detail the mechanics of Chinese versification and the art of translating Chinese poetry. A number of Chinese poems will be taken apart and discussed word by word, line by line, and after a thorough examination of the parts the poem will be assembled in its English translation. Some foreigners have written to ask about the art of translating Chinese poetry. Such a work might supply a present need.

The love of leisure and quiet was one of the main characteristics of our ancient poets. This love was not due to laziness or indolence. Their quest for leisure and quiet was the striving for the attainment of a state or condition wherein and whereby they could enjoy their notion of happiness. Leisure and quiet were but stepping-stones to higher enjoyments. Leisure was the one indispensable requisite for their self-culture and their contemplation of nature.

They obtained their leisure by reducing their wants to a minimum that they might exert the least bodily effort to supply their material needs. In the curtailment of their wants they practised sacrifice and self-denial. Their motto was, "The minimum of effort, the maximum of happiness."

After a perusal of these poems the reader will see how ardently the old Chinese poets loved nature, and how near to her they lived. Every flower and bird, every stream and hill, seemed to have a presiding spirit with which the poet desired to have communion. They loved to climb a mountain and rest beneath the shade, listening to the music of the wind blowing gently through the pines, or watching the play of the sunbeams dancing on the many-faceted ripples of the water. They were fond of boating in moonlit nights or picking flowers in foggy vales without thoughts

·xi·

of home or dinner. They often retired to a secluded monastery in an afternoon to chat with the abbot or join him in meditation. And, catching the old spirit of Cathay, even coolies of the present day can be seen taking their birds in their cages for an outing at early dawn. In the depth of winter the chirp of insects can be heard in a bustling crowd. On inquiry it is revealed that the insect is kept in a little gourd placed in the bosom of the owner. The man supplies warmth to the insect, and the insect pays him back in song. Some minds are born happy. One night I was coming home about twelve o'clock. A ricksha man was pulling his empty vehicle apparently also bound for home, singing a rustic song the words of which I did not catch. He was forgetfulness personified —entirely oblivious of the world and his surroundings. At the moment his aged mother, ragged wife, and hungry children were likely waiting for him and his paltry earnings of the day. His song was more eloquent and impressive than any moral discourse I ever heard. He was then welling with music, contentment, and happiness beyond words to describe. It dawned upon me that happiness was like health; one must never think of it. Once the attention is directed toward it there must be something wrong. It must be the lack of happiness or health that makes people think of the one or the other. The getting seems to be in the forgetting.

The notes which elucidate certain points in the poems, instead of being printed at the bottom of each page, form a separate part of the book. Footnotes are like subordinate personages taking secondary parts in a play. If they stand in conspicuous places they draw attention away from the principal object.

The chronological tables of the T'ang and Sung dynasties will help the reader to appreciate more fully the time in history when these poems were written. And lest the Chinese periods of history may mean but little to the Western reader, contemporaneous dates in Western history are supplied by the insertion of the tables of the popes of Rome and the kings of England. The early T'ang period is from A.D. 618 to 827, in which time there was no mention of the kings of England. This gap is filled by the insertion of the tables of the popes of Rome, including the years A.D. 590 to 1281. From A.D. 827 King Egbert of England began to reign.

Some of these translations were published in 1905 by the *East Asia Magazine*, owned by the *North China Daily News* of Shanghai. In 1922 they were overhauled and many defects and errors were found.

To my friend Mr. Leonard A. Lyall, commissioner of Chinese Customs, translator of the *Chung Yung* 中庸, and "Sayings of Confucius" 論語, I am indebted for improvements and suggestions. To Miss Louise Hammond, an American missionary of Wu-sih, who devotes her leisure to Chinese poetry and music, I am indebted for valuable hints and criticism. My thanks are due to H. G. W. Woodhead, Esq., of the *Tientsin Peking Times*, through whose good offices I am granted the permission by Mr. R. W. Davis, present manager of the *North China Daily News*, to reproduce these poems in a revised form. My thanks are due to Dr. L. T. Chen 陳立廷君, secretary of the Central Y.M.C.A. of China, and to Dr. C. Walter Young for encouragement and advice as to publication, the latter kindly undertaking the trouble of seeing the work through the press. Mrs. C. Walter Young has also gone through the original manuscript for the purpose of selecting those poems of greatest interest and appeal to foreign readers. Mr. Huang Po-lien 黃伯廉君 has kindly done all the typing. I take this opportunity to thank Dr. Todani 戶谷銀三郎博士, director and chief physician of the South Manchurian Railway Hospital, and his colleagues for restoring my irregular heart to its normal function and for general improvement in health, without which my work could not have been completed. To my friend Mr. W. R. Langdon, United States consul in Dairen, is due the detection of many errors. There are probably many errors undetected. I shall be grateful if they be pointed out to me so as to have them corrected in the future. And finally, I crave the indulgence of the readers and sympathy of the critics.

PEIPING, CHINA
April 17, 1930

CONTENTS

TITLES OF POEMS	xvii
POEMS	1
NOTES TO POEMS	123
INDEX TO POETS	137
CHRONOLOGICAL TABLES	140
T'ang Dynasty, A.D. 618–906	140
Sung Dynasty, A.D. 960–1279	141
Popes and Bishops of Rome, A.D. 590–1281	141
Kings of England, A.D. 827–1399	145

TITLES OF POEMS

1. Sleeping in Spring 1
2. Calling on Yüan the Censor 2
3. Farewell to Kwo 3
4. The Lo-yang Road 4
5. Alone on the Ching-t'ing Hills 5
6. Ascending the Heron Tower 6
7. Lines to Princess Yung Lo, Bride of a Tartar Prince . . . 7
8. A Yi-chou Song 8
9. Pear Blossoms in the Palace 9
10. Yearning for the King 10
11. At Mr. Yüan's Garden 11
12. Farewell to Chao Tsung at Night 12
13. In a Summer-House among the Bamboos 13
14. Farewell to Chu Ta Who Goes to Ch'in 14
15. A Ch'ang Kan (Nanking) Song 15
16. A Historical Incident 16
17. Written after Retiring as Minister of State 17
18. Meeting a Heroic Person 18
19. View of the K'wang-lu Mountains from the Yangtze River . 19
20. Replying to Li Han 20
21. Autumn Song 21
22. Lines to Ch'iu Written at Night 22
23. An Autumn Day 23
24. Autumn on the Lake 24
25. An Emperor's Poem 25

·xvii·

26. Calling on a Hermit 26
27. Autumn on the River Fen 27
28. Delay on the Sze-ch'uan Road 28
29. Midnight Thoughts 29
30. A Ch'iu P'u Song 30
31. Lines to Ch'iao, Vice-President 31
32. To the Governor of Wu-ling 32
33. A Soldier's Thought of Home 33
34. Chieh Yü's Complaint 34
35. The Bamboo Grove Monastery 35
36. Lines in Ch'ü Yüan's Temple 36
37. Farewell by the River Yi 37
38. Farewell to Lu Ch'in-ch'ing 38
39. A Reply 39
40. Impromptu Lines on a Spring Day 40
41. A Day in Spring 41
42. A Spring Evening 42
43. Early Spring in the Eastern Suburb 43
44. An Early Shower in Spring 44
45. New Year's Day 45
46. Court Feast in the First Full Moon of the New Year . . . 46
47. Verses Written on the Painting of a Polo Match . . . 47
48. A Palace Song 48
49. A Palace Examination 49
50. Expecting Her Husband's Return 50
51. An Impromptu Verse 51
52. Lines to the Crabapple 52
53. All Souls' Day 53
54. Feast to the Dead 54
55. A Rural Festival Day 55
56. Fasting Day 56

·xviii·

57. Spring in South China 57
58. To Kao P'ing, Undersecretary 58
59. A Pleasant Stroll 59
60. Trying to Visit a Garden 60
61. A Traveler's Song 61
62. Lines on a Screen 62
63. A Quiet Scene 63
64. The Peach Blossoms of Hsüan-tu Temple 64
65. Second Visit to the Hsüan-tu Temple 65
66. A Ferry West of Ch'u-chou 66
67. Shadows of Flowers 67
68. The Northern Hills 68
69. On the Lake 69
70. A Quiet Day 70
71. A Clear Day in Spring 71
72. Late Spring 72
73. A Stroll in the Garden Late in Spring 73
74. The Weaving Orioles 74
75. Departed Spring 75
76. Climbing the Hills 76
77. The Cocoon Woman's Song 77
78. End of Spring 78
79. Grieving over the Passing of Spring 79
80. Farewell to Spring 80
81. The Last Eve of Spring 81
82. Beginning of Summer when away from Home . . . 82
83. The Appointed Hour 83
84. Rising from a Summer Nap 84
85. On the Ch'u-chou Road 85
86. The Passing Moment 86
87. A Summer Day 87

88. Evening Scene from a Balcony 88
89. Summer in a Mountain Retreat 89
90. A Farmer's Home 90
91. A Rural Scene 91
92. Lines to the Pomegranate Flowers 92
93. The Thatched Eaves 93
94. Wu Yi or Swallows' Lane 94
95. Farewell to an Envoy to Kucha 95
96. Lines on a Memorial Tablet 96
97. Lines Written in Hwai-nan Temple 97
98. Autumn 98
99. Evening of the Seventh Day of the Seventh Moon 99
100. Beginning of Autumn 100
101. An Autumn Eve 101
102. Mid-Autumn 102
103. Sadness on Ascending a Tower by the River Bank . . 103
104. The West Lake 104
105. A West Lake View in July 105
106. Rain on the West Lake 106
107. On Duty at Court 107
108. A Pavilion by the Water 108
109. In the Forbidden Court 109
110. Reflection after Reading 110
111. The Floated Ship 111
112. To the Mountain Brook 112
113. A Winter Scene 113
114. Anchored at Night by the Maple Bridge 114
115. A Cold Night 115
116. The Two Fairies 116
117. The Plum Trees' Complaint 117
118. Early Spring 118

·XX·

119. THE SNOW AND PLUM-FLOWERS' RIVALRY 119

120. THE SNOW AND PLUM-FLOWERS 120

121. REPLY TO CHUNG JO-WENG 121

122. ANCHORED AT NIGHT IN THE CH'IN-HWAI DISTRICT (NANKING) . . 122

Poems from No. 1 to No. 39 are of five words in each line, forming one section.

Poems from No. 40 to No. 122 are of seven words in the line, forming another section.

Both sections of the poems were arranged by the original compiler, Hsieh Fang-te, according to the seasons. This fact will explain why poem No. 40 and a few that follow have anew spring as their subject.

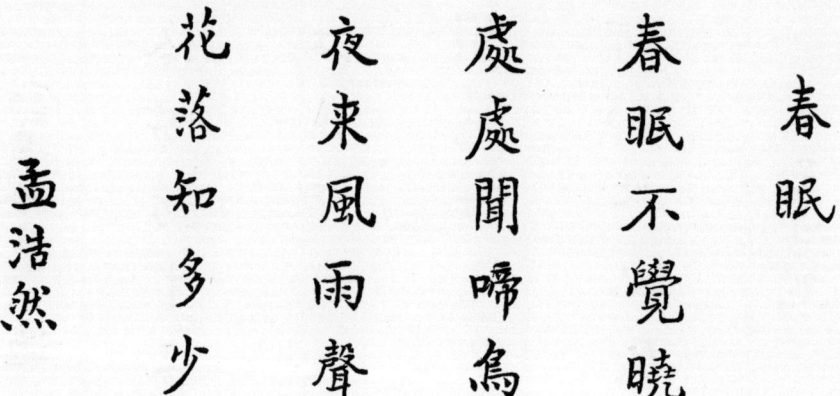

1

SLEEPING IN SPRING

I slept in spring, unconscious of the dawn,
When songs of birds were heard on every lawn;
At night came sounds of rain and wind that blew,
How many a blossom fell there no one knew!

MENG HAO-JAN

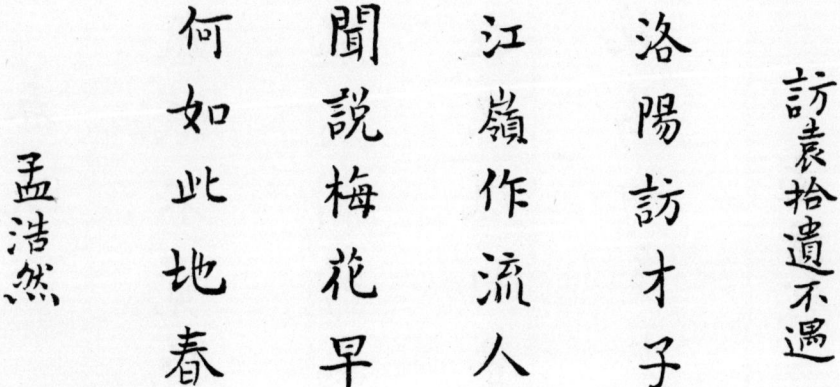

訪袁拾遺不遇

洛陽訪才子
江嶺作流人
聞說梅花早
何如此地春

孟浩然

2

CALLING ON YÜAN THE CENSOR

On thee at Lo-yang did I call, good friend,
Thy exile days o'er Chiang-ling thou wilt spend.
'Tis said the plum-trees blossom early there,
But spring at home to thee must seem more fair!

MENG HAO-JAN

送郭司倉

映門淮水綠
留騎主人心
明月隨良掾
春潮夜夜深

王昌齡

3

FAREWELL TO KWO

The Hwai's blue stream may quickly pass my door,
But thou must longer stay I now implore;
The shining moon will light thy journey home,
Deep floods of spring each eve to me will come.

WANG CH'ANG-LING

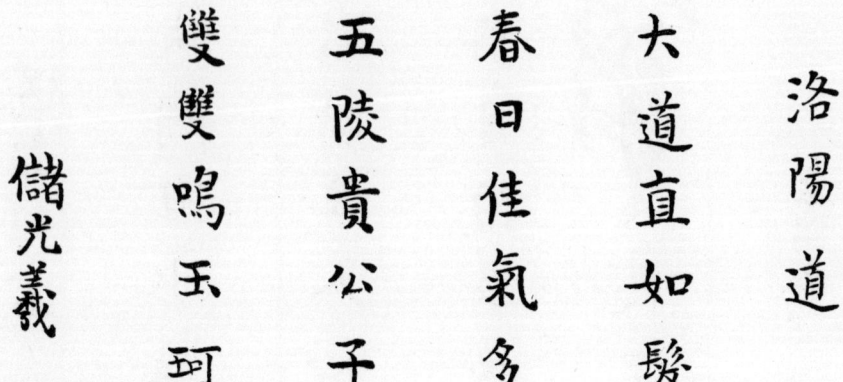

4

THE LO-YANG ROAD

The Lo-yang highway runs as straight as hair,
And when the days in spring are bright and fair,
The Wu-ling princes thither go to race,
Their trappings' jingling music mark their pace.

CH'U KWANG-HSI

獨坐敬亭山

眾鳥高飛盡
孤雲獨去閒
相看兩不厭
只有敬亭山

李白

5

ALONE ON THE CHING-T'ING HILLS

The birds have flown away on pinions high,
A cloud in heedless mood goes floating by.
The two that never change their fixed regard,
Are ye, fair Ching-t'ing Hills, and I, your bard.

LI PO

·5·

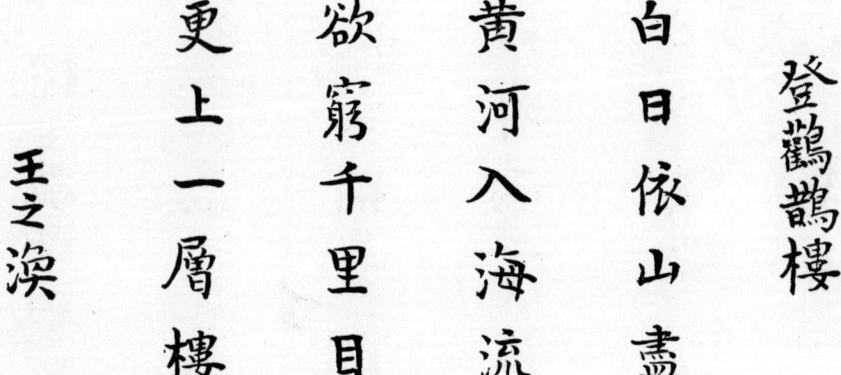

6

ASCENDING THE HERON TOWER

The sun behind the western hills now glows,
And toward the sea the Yellow River flows.
Wish you an endless view to cheer your eyes?
Then one more story mount and higher rise.

WANG CHIH-HUAN

·6·

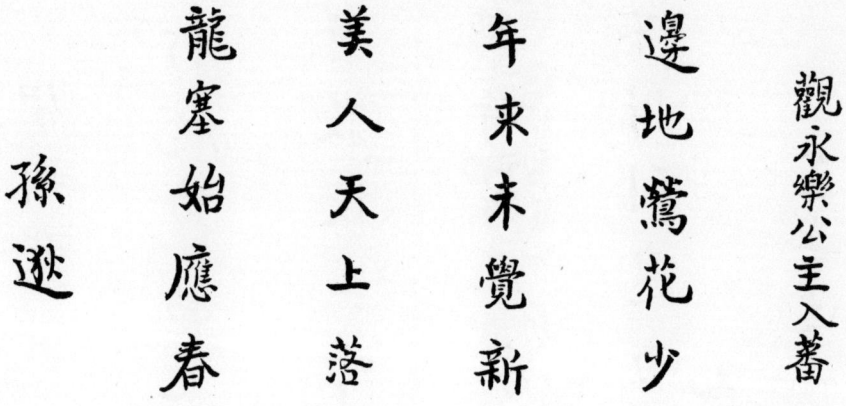

7

LINES TO PRINCESS YUNG-LO, BRIDE OF A TARTAR PRINCE

Those borders wild no birds or blossoms cheer,
And late the year when signs of spring appear.
Our Princess, angel-like, will there descend,
To tardy spring her maiden beauty lend.

SUN TI

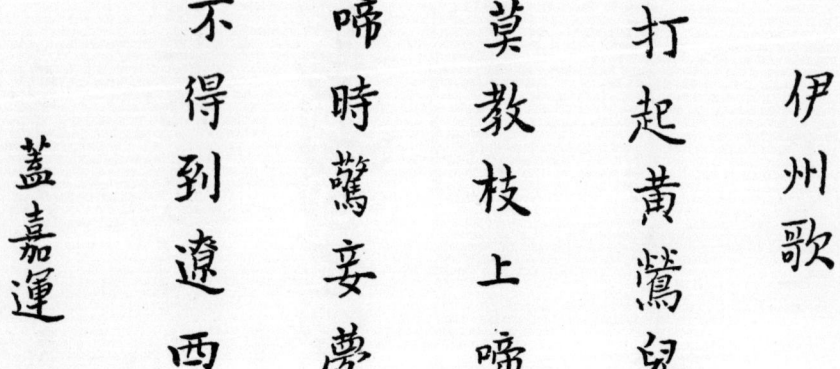

伊州歌

打起黃鶯兒
莫教枝上啼
啼時驚妾夢
不得到遼西

蓋嘉運

A YI-CHOU SONG

Oh drive the orioles off,
    Nor let them warble on the tree!
Their warblings wake my dream,
    In Liao-hsi I will never be!

KAI CHIA-YÜN

左掖梨花

冷艷全欺雪
餘香乍入衣
春風且莫定
吹向玉階飛

丘為

9

PEAR-BLOSSOMS IN THE PALACE

Thy spotless beauty puts to shame the snow,
Thy perfume through the royal robe shall go.
Uncertain tho' may seem the winds of spring,
Thy petals waft directly to the King!

CH'IU WEI

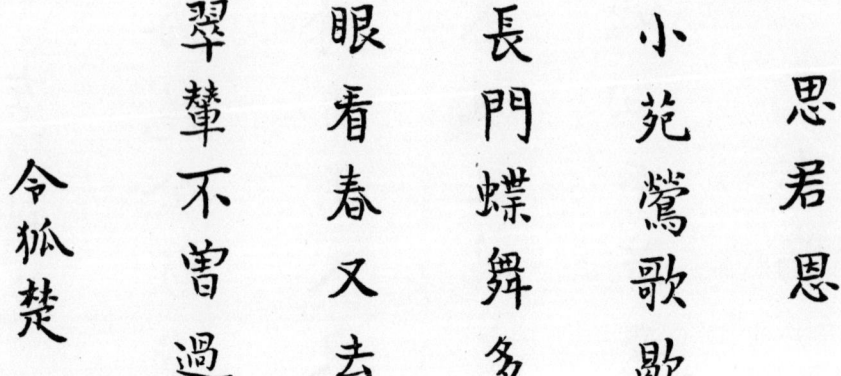

思君恩

小苑鶯歌歇

長門蝶舞多

眼看春又去

翠輦不曾過

令狐楚

YEARNING FOR THE KING

The orioles in the garden sing no more,
The butterflies now flit about my door.
As fades the spring my days are fading fast,
My door the royal chariot never passed.

LING-HU CH'U

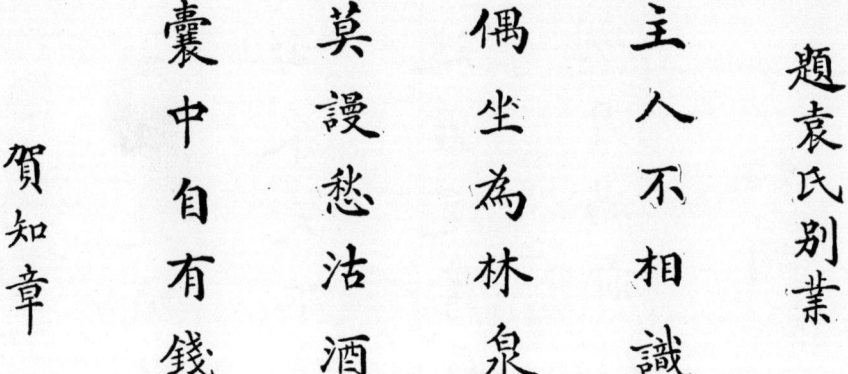

AT MR. YÜAN'S GARDEN

The landlord here may know me not,
Chance brings me to this charming spot;
Nor fear I'll fail to pay for wine,
Within the purse the coins are mine.

Ho Chih-chang

·11·

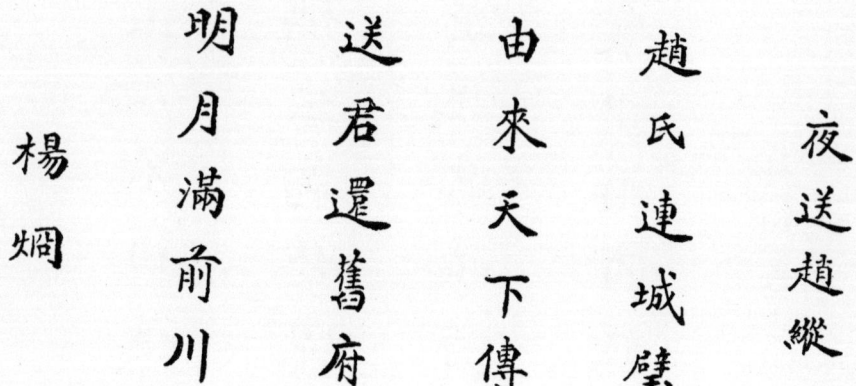

夜送趙縱

趙氏連城璧

由來天下傳

送君還舊府

明月滿前川

楊烱

12

FAREWELL TO CHAO TSUNG AT NIGHT

The state of Chao the rarest gem possessed,
The fame of which the world had long confessed.
Do thou of equal fame go home this night,
Whilst yonder stream is full of moonbeams bright.

YANG CH'IUNG

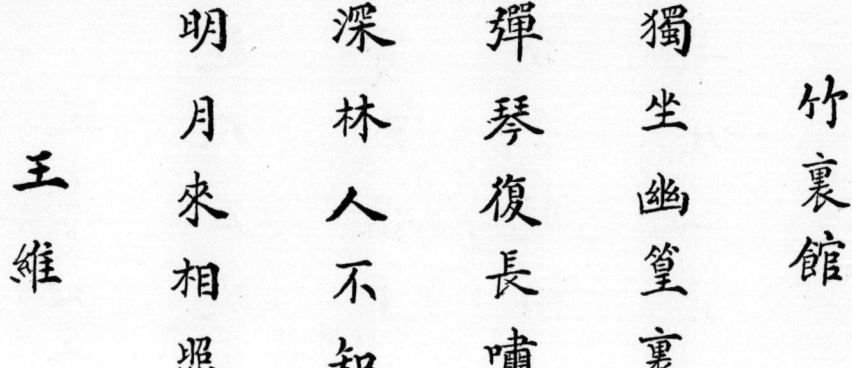

竹裏館

獨坐幽篁裏
彈琴復長嘯
深林人不知
明月來相照

王維

13

IN A SUMMER-HOUSE AMONG THE BAMBOOS

Alone I sat beneath the bamboos' shade,
And hummed an air, whilst on the lute I played,
Unseen by all within the thicket deep,
Except the shining moon that came to peep.

WANG WEI

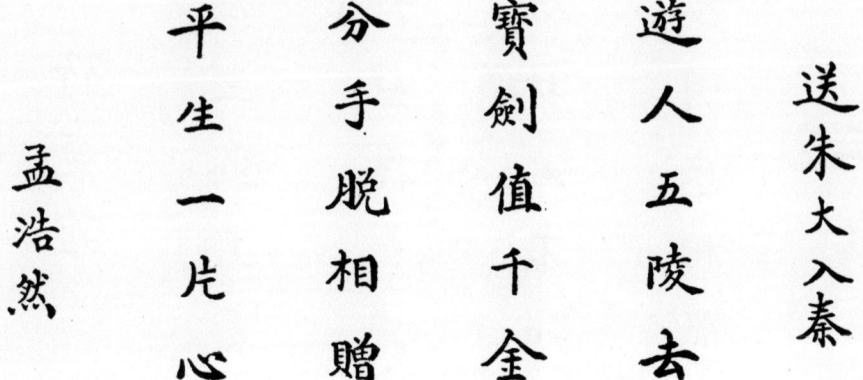

送朱大入秦

遊人五陵去
寶劍值千金
分手脫相贈
平生一片心

孟浩然

FAREWELL TO CHU TA WHO GOES
TO CH'IN

Oh friend, if thou to Wu-ling yet must go,
This sword of priceless worth to thee I show,
And as a parting present give to thee,
To mark our friendship's loyal constancy.

MENG HAO-JAN

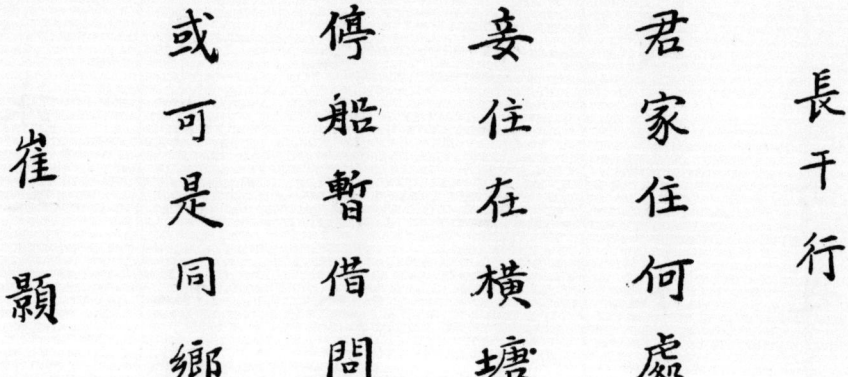

長干行

君家住何處

妾住在橫塘

停船暫借問

或可是同鄉

崔顥

15

A CH'ANG-KAN (NANKING) SONG

O Mister, where's thy home, I pray?
I live in Heng-t'ang, close this way.
I stop the boat to ask of thee,
Perchance we fellow-townsmen be.

Ts'ui Hao

·15·

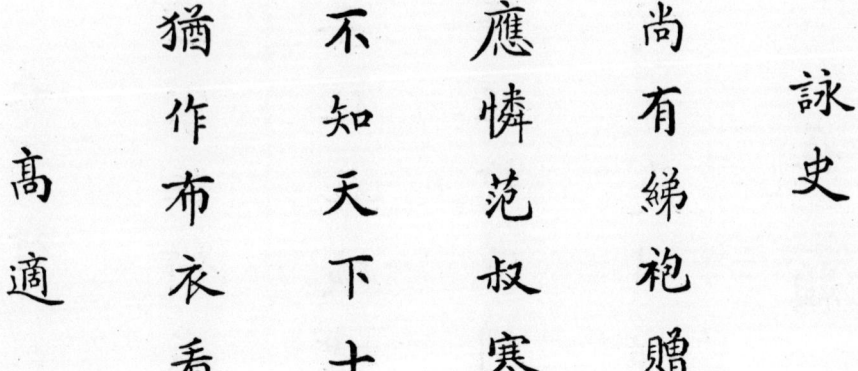

詠史

尚有綈袍贈
應憐范叔寒
不知天下士
猶作布衣看

高適

16

A HISTORICAL INCIDENT

Hsü still can give a robe in sympathy
    To pity Fan who looks exceeding cold.
Hsü knows him not a minister of state,
    But takes him for the same poor friend of old.

KAO SHIH

罷相作

避賢初罷相

樂聖且銜杯

為問門前客

今朝幾個來

李適之

17

WRITTEN AFTER RETIRING AS MINISTER OF STATE

To worthier hands I leave the rule of state,
    T'enjoy my wine and while my time away.
Of those who once came crowding at the gate
    A few may now appear at early day.

LI SHIH-CHIH

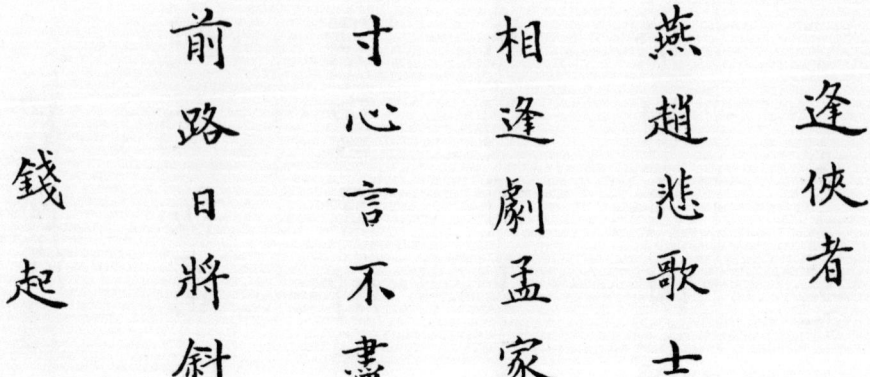

逢俠者

燕趙悲歌士
相逢劇孟家
寸心言不盡
前路日將斜

錢起

18

MEETING A HEROIC PERSON

From Yen or Chao art thou a hero true,
In Chi Meng's home there met by chance we two.
But ere we finish what we have to say,
The setting sun will part again our way.

CH'IEN CH'I

·18·

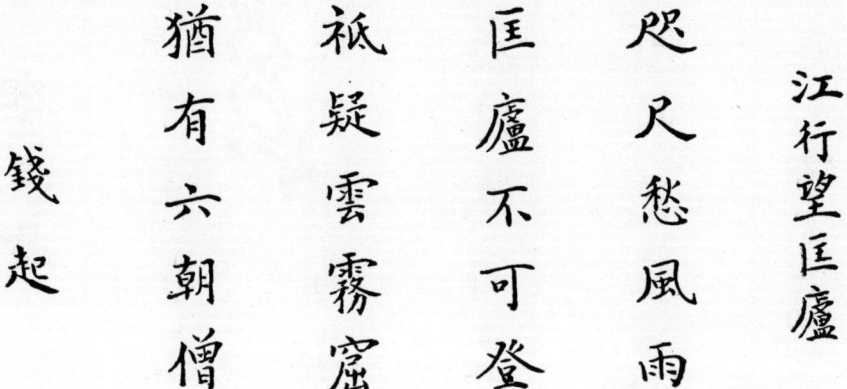

江行望匡廬

咫尺愁風雨

匡廬不可登

祇疑雲霧窟

猶有六朝僧

錢起

19

VIEW OF THE K'WANG-LU MOUNTAINS
FROM THE YANGTZE RIVER

To come so near and then by wind and rain
Be stopped from climbing K'wang-lu's storm-girt chain!
Among those caves, may be, 'mid clouds and mist,
Some monks of realms forgotten still persist.

CH'IEN CH'I

·19·

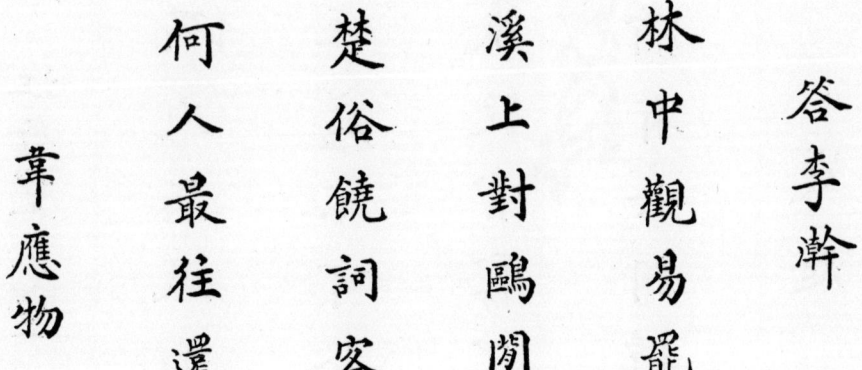

20

REPLYING TO LI HAN

My leisure in a grove the classics lull,
Or by a stream I watch an idle gull.
The state of Ch'u has men of talents rare,
'Mong them, whose closest friendship do you share?

WEI YING-WU

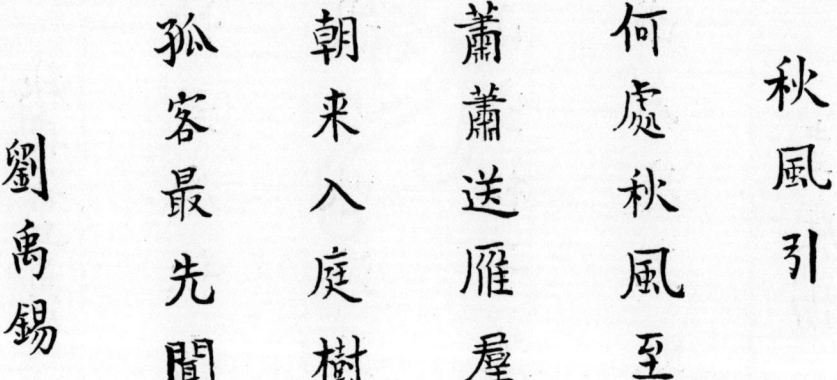

21

AUTUMN SONG

Oh, whence this autumn breeze so loud and strong,
Which, whirring, drives the migrant geese along?
Its moan among the garden trees at morn
I'm first to hear, a wanderer forlorn.

LIU YÜ-HSI

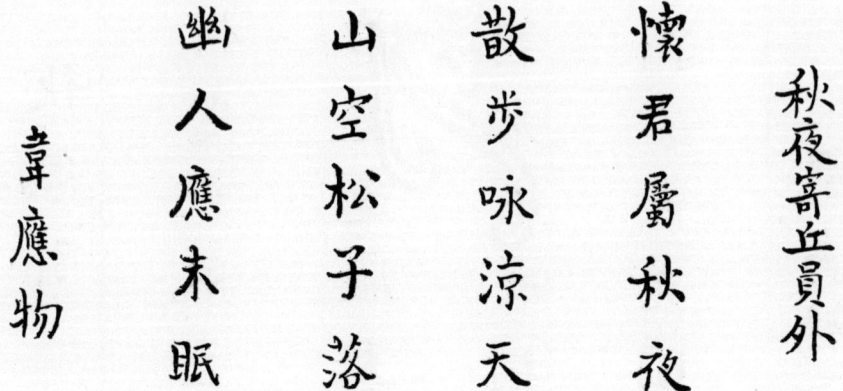

秋夜寄丘員外

懷君屬秋夜
散步詠涼天
山空松子落
幽人應未眠

韋應物

22

LINES TO CH'IU WRITTEN AT NIGHT

My thoughts are gone to thee this autumn night.
I pace and hum beneath the cool moonlight.
The pine-cones fall 'mid mountain silence deep.
Art thou, my hermit friend, not yet asleep?

WEI YING-WU

秋日

返照入閭巷
憂來誰共語
古道少人行
秋風動禾黍

耿湋

AN AUTUMN DAY

The setting sun lights up the village lane.
　I'm sad but who will come to entertain?
The ancient roads are shunned by passing folk,
　While winds of autumn rock the ripening grain.

KENG WEI

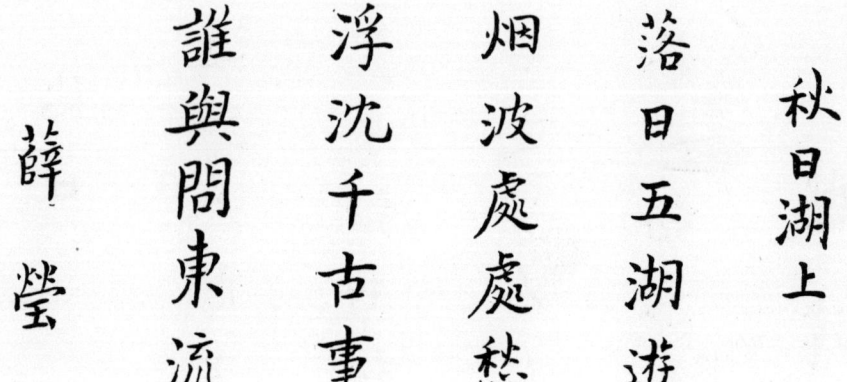

秋日湖上

落日五湖遊

烟波處處愁

浮沈千古事

誰與問東流

薛瑩

AUTUMN ON THE LAKE

At sunset on the T'ai-hu Lake we sailed,
A gloomy sadness o'er the waves prevailed.
Here rose and fell full many an ancient state,
Like streams that eastward flow—who asks their fate?

HSIEH YUNG

宮中題

輦路生秋草

上林花滿枝

憑高何限意

無復侍臣知

文宗皇帝

25

AN EMPEROR'S POEM

The royal walks are choked with autumn weeds,
The royal garden full of flowering trees.
Though on a throne, I'm moved by other thoughts
Unknown to courtiers who attend to me.

EMPEROR WEN TSUNG
T'ang Dynasty

尋隱者不遇

松下問童子
言師採藥去
只在此山中
雲深不知處

賈島

CALLING ON A HERMIT

I asked a lad beneath an old pine tree—
"My master's gone for herbs," he said to me.
"He must be here within this mountain dell,
   But where, with clouds so thick, I cannot tell."

CHIA TAO

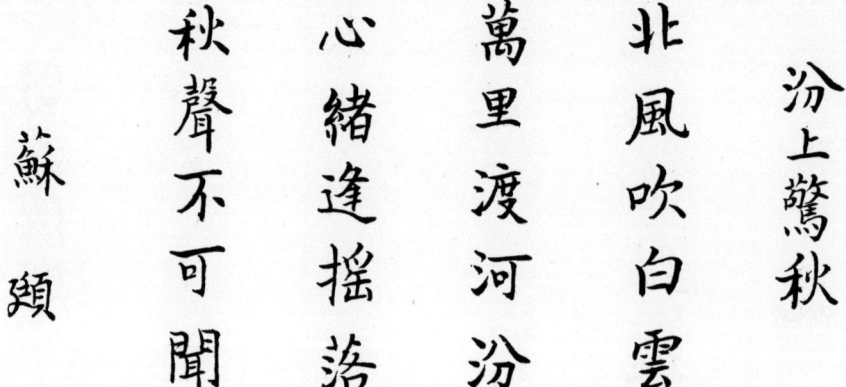

27

AUTUMN ON THE RIVER FEN

White clouds are scudding while the north winds blow.
Far, far, beyond the river Fen I go.
My heart is trembling like a falling leaf,
As autumn's voice I hear with bitter grief.

SU T'ING

蜀道後期

客心爭日月

來往預期程

秋風不相待

先至洛陽城

張說

28

DELAY ON THE SZE-CH'UAN ROAD

We're pressing home and moments precious seem,
Each stage is ready planned along the way.
But autumn winds for me will not delay,
So you will get to Lo-yang first, I deem.

CHANG YÜEH

·28·

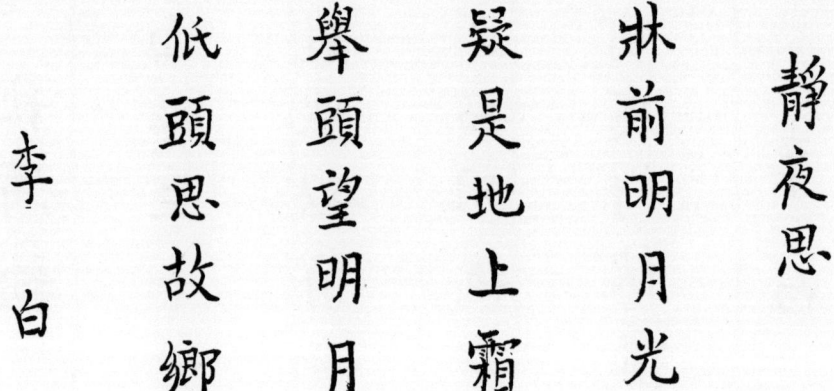

靜夜思

牀前明月光
疑是地上霜
舉頭望明月
低頭思故鄉

李白

MIDNIGHT THOUGHTS

My bed was radiant with a shining light
Which I, in wonder, took for frost so bright.
With upraised head the shining moon I spied,
With drooping head I thought of home and sighed.

Li Po

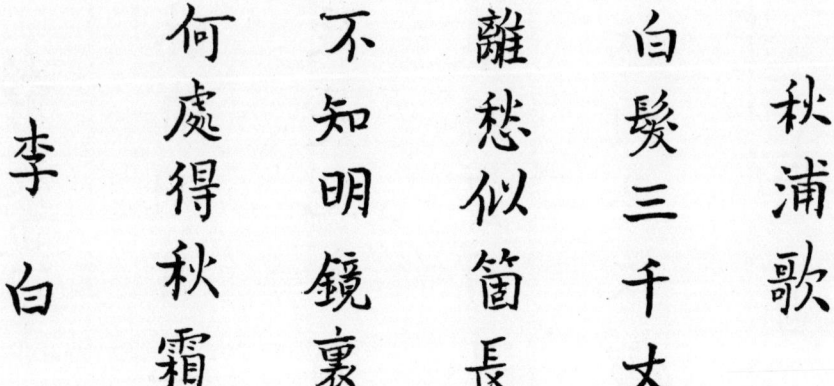

30

A CH'IU P'U SONG

How long my whitened locks appear to me!
How deep my parting sorrow seems to be!
I wonder, too, within the mirror bright,
Whence comes this autumn frost to sadden sight!

L<small>I</small> Po

贈喬侍郎

漢庭榮巧宦
雲閣薄邊功
可憐驄馬使
白首為誰雄

陳子昂

31

LINES TO CH'IAO, VICE-PRESIDENT

The court of Han but cravens glorified,
And our heroic warriors cast aside.
I pity thee, the nation's "Noble Steed,"
Why toil with silver locks when none takes heed?

CH'EN TZǓ-ANG

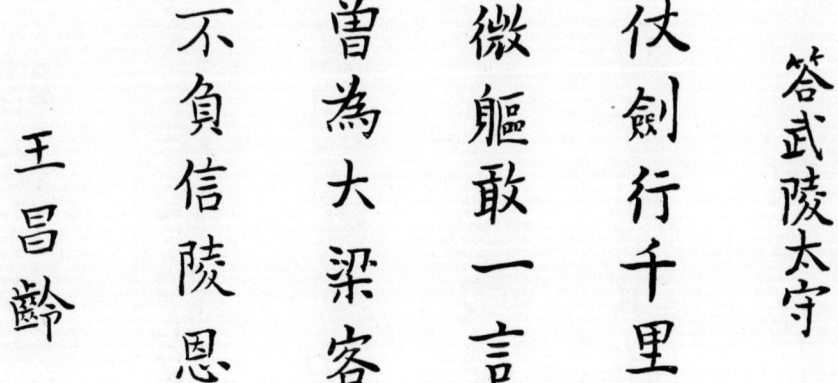

答武陵太守

仗劍行千里
微軀敢一言
曾為大梁客
不負信陵恩

王昌齡

32

TO THE GOVERNOR OF WU-LING

With trusty blade I came a thousand *li*.
Dare I withhold my grateful words from thee?
Like Ta-liang's honored guest have I been met,
Like Hsin-ling's bounty, thine, I'll ne'er forget!

WANG CH'ANG-LING

·32·

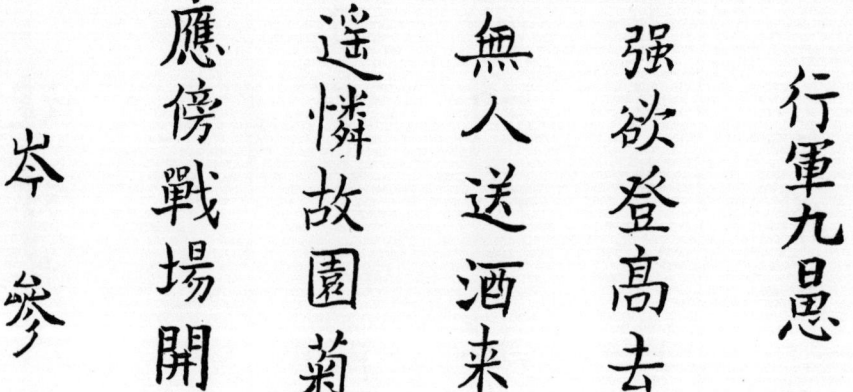

行軍九日思
強欲登高去
無人送酒來
遙憐故園菊
應傍戰場開
岑參

33

A SOLDIER'S THOUGHT OF HOME
Ninth Day of the Ninth Month (October)

Oh, how I yearn to climb some mountain height,
But none provides the wine that gives delight.
Ah, those chrysanthemums at home, I fear,
A battlefield, perhaps, are blooming near.

TS'EN TS'AN

婕妤怨

花枝出建章

鳳管發昭陽

借問承恩者

雙蛾幾許長

皇甫冉

34

CHIEH YÜ'S COMPLAINT

A beauty to the palace winds her way,
And from the court come sounds of music gay.
Oh, say, thou who hast royal favors known,
Have all thy lovely charms now sweeter grown?

HUANG-FU JAN

·34·

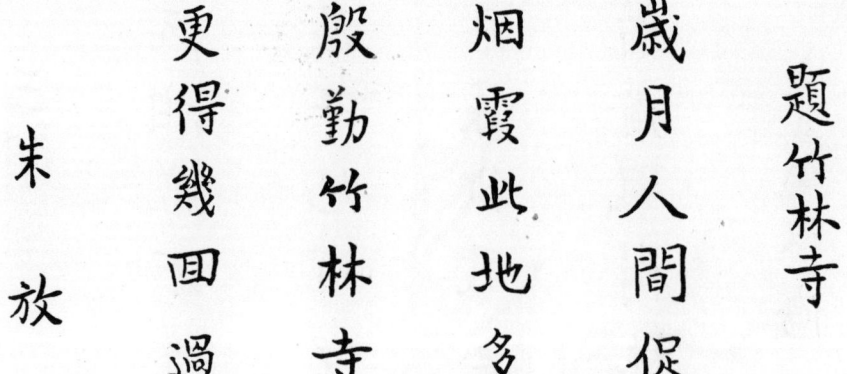

題竹林寺

歲月人間促

烟霞此地多

殷勤竹林寺

更得幾回過

朱放

35

THE BAMBOO GROVE MONASTERY

Time presses mortals on with quickened speed,
But here alluring sights in turn succeed,
As hospitality would urge me stay,
I linger, since I seldom pass this way.

CHU FANG

三閭廟

沅湘流不盡
屈子怨何深
日暮秋風起
蕭蕭楓樹林

戴叔倫

36

LINES IN CH'Ü YÜAN'S TEMPLE

Like floods of Yüan and Hsiang that ever flow,
Thy endless grief, O Ch'ü Yüan, who shall know?
At evening comes the autumn's moaning breeze
To weep for thee among the maple trees.

TAI SHU-LUN

易水送別

此地別燕丹

壯士髮衝冠

昔時人已沒

今日水猶寒

駱賓王

FAREWELL BY THE RIVER YI

'Twas here that prince and hero farewell said.
That dauntless hero proudly held his head.
Those valiant men of old have passed away,
Still trembling flows this icy stream today.

Lo Pin-wang

別盧秦卿

知有前期在

難分此夜中

無將故人酒

不及石尤風

司空曙

38

FAREWELL TO LU CH'IN-CH'ING

Full well I know we yet shall meet again,
    But this night's parting long would I detain.
Consider not thy old friend's wine so poor,
    That thou must need "deterrent winds" t'remain.

Ssŭ-k'ung Shu

答人

偶来松樹下

高枕石頭眠

山中無曆日

寒盡不知年

太上隱者

A REPLY

By chance I come to rest beneath these pines—
On stony pillow here my head reclines.
Among the hills none marks the passing day,
Or minds how wintry years may roll away.

AN ANCIENT HERMIT

春日偶成

雲淡風輕近午天
傍花隨柳過前川
時人不識余心樂
將謂偷閒學少年

程顥

IMPROMPTU LINES ON A SPRING DAY

In days when clouds are light and breezes softly blow,
I cross to yonder stream where flowers and willows grow.
Some worldlings, knowing not my heart's deep inward joy,
May say I snatch these hours to play the truant boy.

CH'ENG HAO

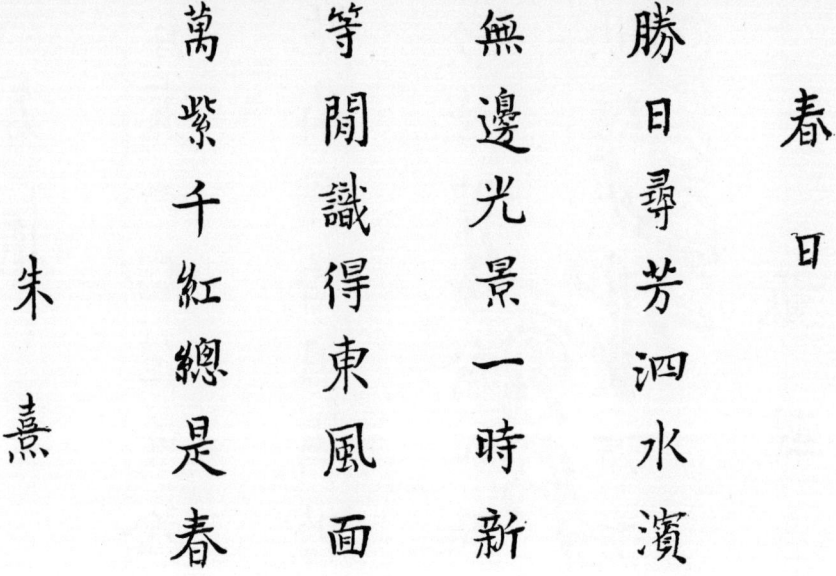

41

A DAY IN SPRING

A perfect day to garner flowers along the Sze,
　Where spreads a boundless prospect altogether new!
I know but slightly how the east wind's face doth look—
　When all is red and purple, spring is surely due.

CHU HSI

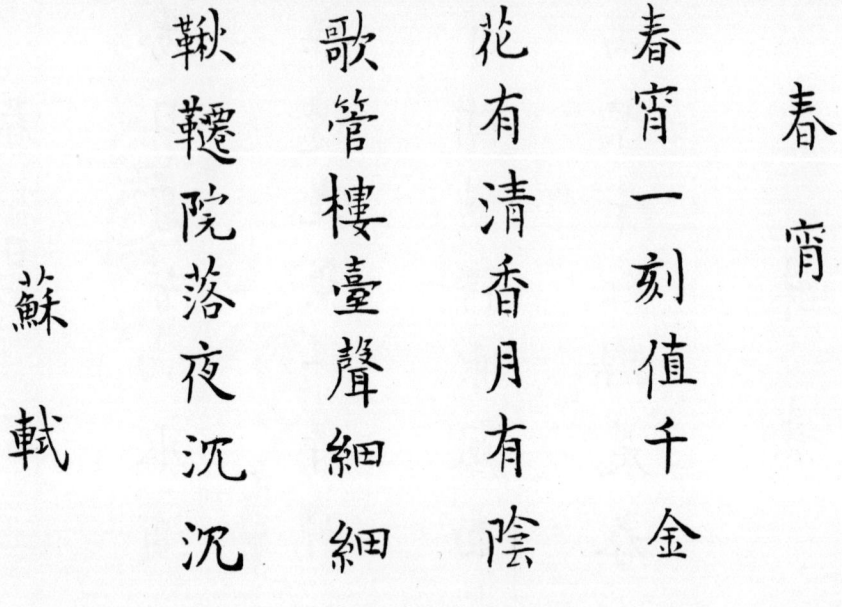

春宵一刻值千金
花有清香月有陰
歌管樓臺聲細細
鞦韆院落夜沉沉

春宵

蘇軾

42

A SPRING EVENING

One eve of spring exceeds the price of finest gold;
Then sheds the moon pure light and flowers their scent unfold,
From banquet halls come strains of joyous music soft,
And maidens happy rock their garden swings aloft.

SU SHIH

城東早春

詩家清景在新春
綠柳纔黄半未勻
若待上林花似錦
出門俱是看花人

楊巨源

EARLY SPRING IN THE EASTERN SUBURB

The signs of early spring attract the poet's eye,
Ere willows' tender yellow turns to greenish dye.
Nor will he wait till tender shrubs in splendor blow,
For then the crowd can also note the floral show.

YANG CHÜ-YÜAN

初春小雨

天街小雨潤如酥
草色遙看近却無
最是一年春好處
絕勝烟柳滿皇都

韓愈

AN EARLY SHOWER IN SPRING

Along the streets the sweet and welcome shower comes,
The green of grass as seen afar is gone when near.
The year's most precious gifts have tokens in the spring,
When willows, hid in mist, above the town appear.

HAN YÜ

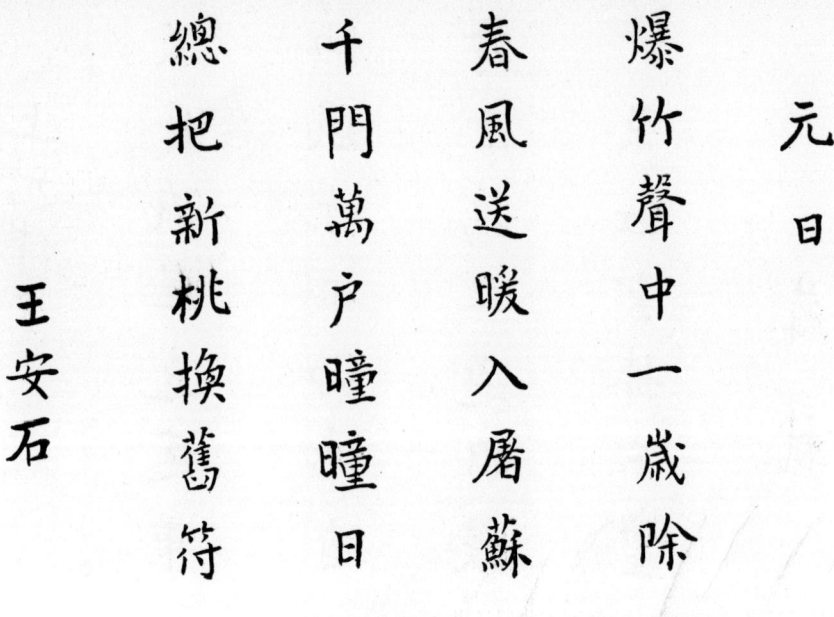

元日

爆竹聲中一歲除
春風送暖入屠蘇
千門萬戶曈曈日
總把新桃換舊符

王安石

NEW YEAR'S DAY

Amid the din of crackers goes the parting year,
  The winds of spring bring warmth to help the wine mature.
To every home the sun imparts its brighter rays,
  Old peachwood charms, renewed, 'gainst evil shall insure.

WANG AN-SHIH

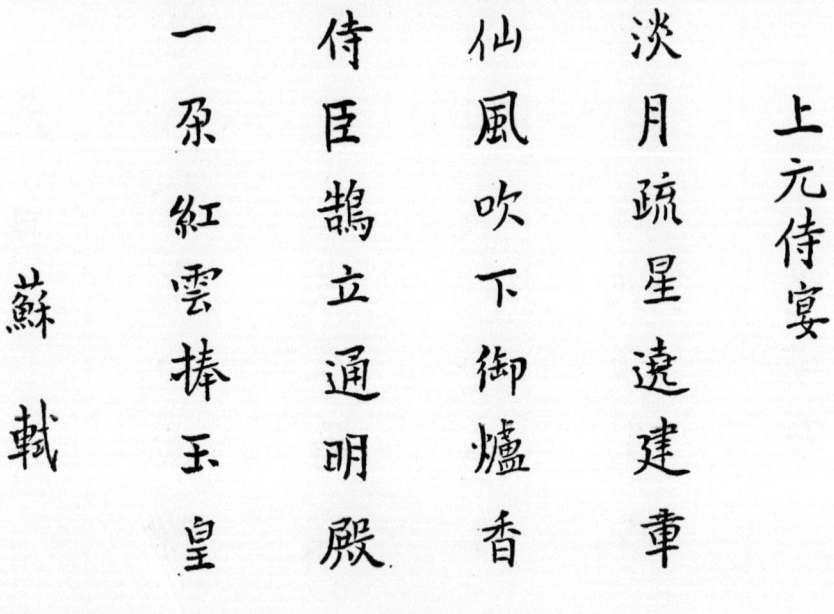

上元侍宴

淡月疏星遠建章
仙風吹下御爐香
侍臣鵠立通明殿
一朵紅雲捧玉皇

蘇軾

46

COURT FEAST IN THE FIRST FULL
MOON OF THE NEW YEAR

The tender moon and scattered stars on Chien-chang shine,
The gentle wind bestirs the smoke of incense fine,
While courtiers stand erect around their monarch proud,
Who seems a god enthroned upon a purple cloud.

SU SHIH

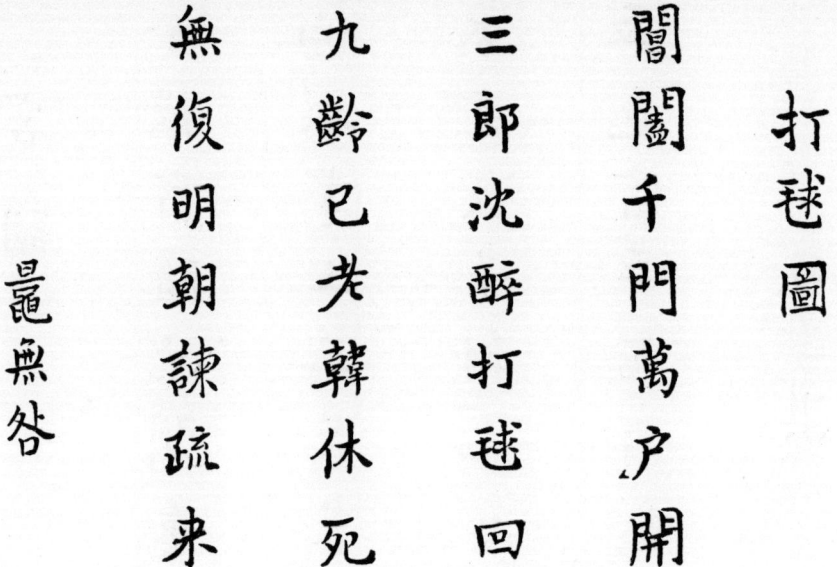

47

VERSES WRITTEN ON THE PAINTING
OF A POLO MATCH

Wide stand the gates and doors throughout the central court—
The drunken monarch now returns from polo sport.
Chiu-ling is now retired, Han Hsiu to death has gone,
When morn appears, reproofs that come shall be withdrawn.

CH'AO WU-CHIU

宮詞

金殿當頭紫閣重

仙人掌上玉芙蓉

太平天子朝元日

五色雲車駕六龍

林淇

48

A PALACE SONG

The palace stands in front with purple courts around,
Upon th' Immortal's palm a sacred bowl is found;
The monarch goes, in peace, to pray in New Year's dawn.
His gorgeous chariot moves, by six fine horses drawn.

LIN CH'I

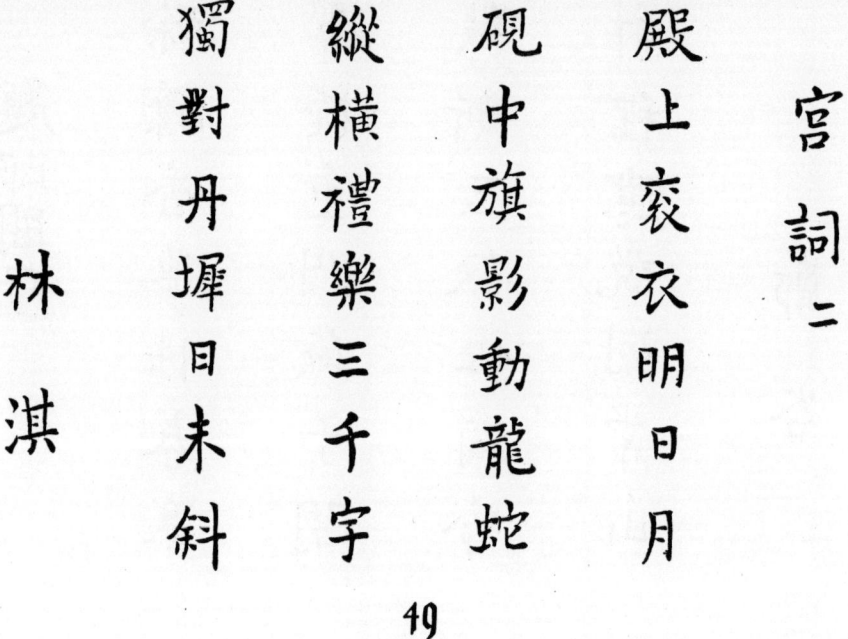

宮詞二

殿上袞衣明日月
硯中旗影動龍蛇
縱橫禮樂三千字
獨對丹墀日未斜

林淇

THE PALACE EXAMINATION
(A Palace Song No. 2)

In gorgeous dress the monarch took the throne,
   Like sun or moon his countenance appeared.
The royal standards in my ink-slab shone
   With imaged snakes and 'broidered dragons weird.
Our theme was ancient rites and music old,
In lengthy essays each must then unfold.
When singled out at court, I answer made,
Ere yet the slanting rays could westward fade.

LIN CH'I

題邸間壁

醞釀香夢怯春寒

翠掩重門燕子間

敲斷玉釵紅燭冷

計程應說到常山

鄭谷

50

EXPECTING HER HUSBAND'S RETURN

The spring is cold, though perfumed roses lull my dream.
Inclosed in bowers, an idle swallow I but seem.
The lamp-wick's trimmed, yet chilly burns my candlelight.
By stages timed, Ch'ang-shan should come within his sight.

CHENG KU

絕句

兩個黃鸝鳴翠柳
一行白鷺上青天
窗含西嶺千秋雪
門泊東吳萬里船

杜甫

AN IMPROMPTU VERSE

A pair of orioles sing amid the willows green.
    And up the sky a flock of herons white now soar.
Westward the snow-capped peaks are through my windows seen.
    While junks from far-off Tung-wu lie beyond my door.

TU FU

海棠

東風嫋嫋泛崇光

香霧空濛月轉廊

只恐夜深花睡去

故燒高燭照紅粧

蘇軾

52

LINES TO THE CRABAPPLE

The east wind softly blows but faint is "heaven's torch,"
Which through the perfumed mist is circling round the porch.
And lest my beauty go to sleep at depth of night,
Her radiant form I cheer with lofty candlelight.

SU SHIH

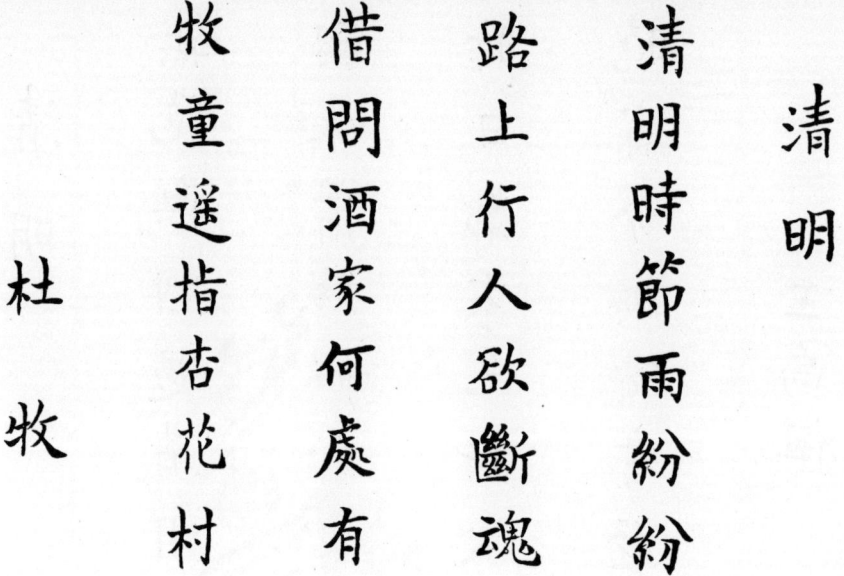

清明

清明時節雨紛紛
路上行人欲斷魂
借問酒家何處有
牧童遙指杏花村

杜牧

53

ALL SOULS' DAY

The rain falls thick and fast on All Souls' festive day,
The men and women sadly move along the way.
They ask where wineshops can be found or where to rest—
And there the herdboy's fingers Almond-Town suggest.

TU MU

·53·

清明

無花無酒過清明
興味蕭然似野僧
昨日鄰家乞新火
曉窗分與讀書燈

王禹偁

54

FEAST TO THE DEAD

This festive day I passed with neither wine nor flowers,
And like a rustic monk I spent the joyless hours.
I asked a neighbor yesterday for new-made light,
The dawn and lamp both made my study doubly bright.

WANG YÜ-CH'ENG

社日

鵝湖山下稻粱肥
豚柵雞棲對掩扉
桑柘影斜春社散
家家扶得醉人歸

張演

55

A RURAL FESTIVAL DAY

Along the O-hu Hills there wave the swelling crops.
  The pigs and fowls are penned against the festive day.
When trees their slanting shadows cast, the feasting stops,
  And homeward tipsy farmers totter on the way.

CHANG YEN

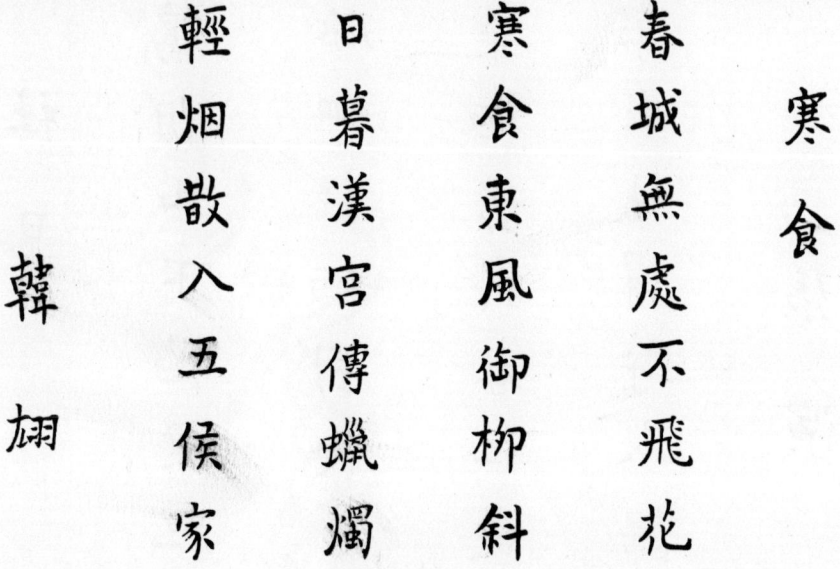

寒食

春城無處不飛花
寒食東風御柳斜
日暮漢宮傳蠟燭
輕烟散入五侯家

韓翃

56

FASTING DAY

Throughout the royal city fly the flowers of spring,
On Fasting Day before the breeze the willows swing.
At dusk the court of Han will waxen candles send
To nobles' homes, where light and incense softly blend.

HAN HUNG

江南春

十里鶯啼綠映紅
水村山郭酒旗風
南朝四百八十寺
多少樓臺烟雨中

杜牧

57

SPRING IN SOUTH CHINA

Through miles of red and green I hear the orioles' notes,
In towns by hills and streams the liquor-banner floats.
Many a Southern Dynasty's temple can be seen
And lofty towers, beyond the rainy, misty screen.

                                        TU MU

上高侍郎

天上碧桃和露種

日邊紅杏倚雲栽

芙蓉生在秋江上

不向東風怨未開

高蟾

58

TO KAO P'ING, UNDERSECRETARY

A sacred peach that waxes green with heaven's dew,
An apricot favored by sun and clouds are you.
But I, hibiscus, by a stream, for autumn wait,
Nor blame the tardy east wind that I blossom late.

KAO CH'AN

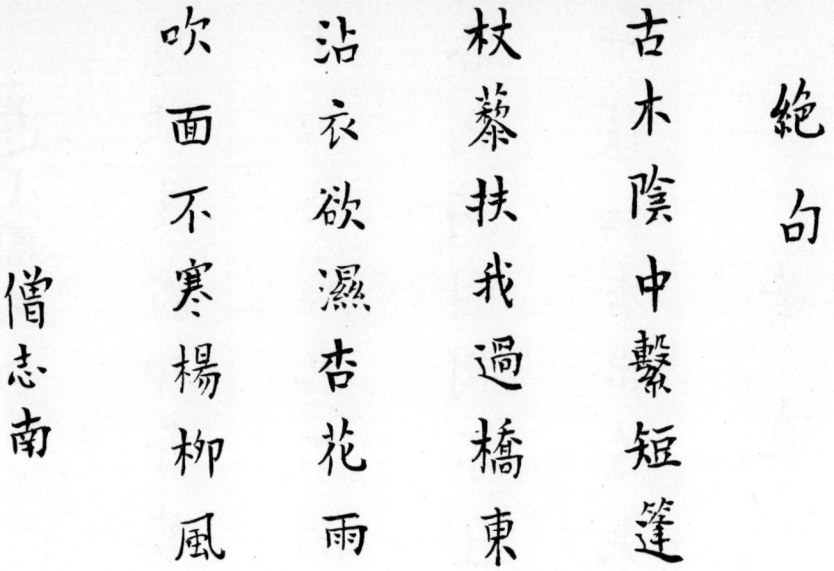

絶句

古木陰中繫短篷

杖藜扶我過橋東

沾衣欲濕杏花雨

吹面不寒楊柳風

僧志南

A PLEASANT STROLL

My boat I moored beneath the ancient forest shade,
With staff in hand I crossed a bridge and eastward strayed.
I felt the shower that cheered the flowering apricot,
The breeze that rocked the swaying willows chilled me not.

CHI NAN
A Buddhist Priest

遊小園不值

應嫌屐齒印蒼苔
十扣柴扉九不開
春色滿園關不住
一枝紅杏出牆來

葉適

60

TRYING TO VISIT A GARDEN

Though knocks I give, no owner at the gate is seen,
I fear my pointed clogs may mar his mossy green.
But charms of spring within a garden who can keep?
A spray of apricot across the wall doth peep!

YEH SHIH

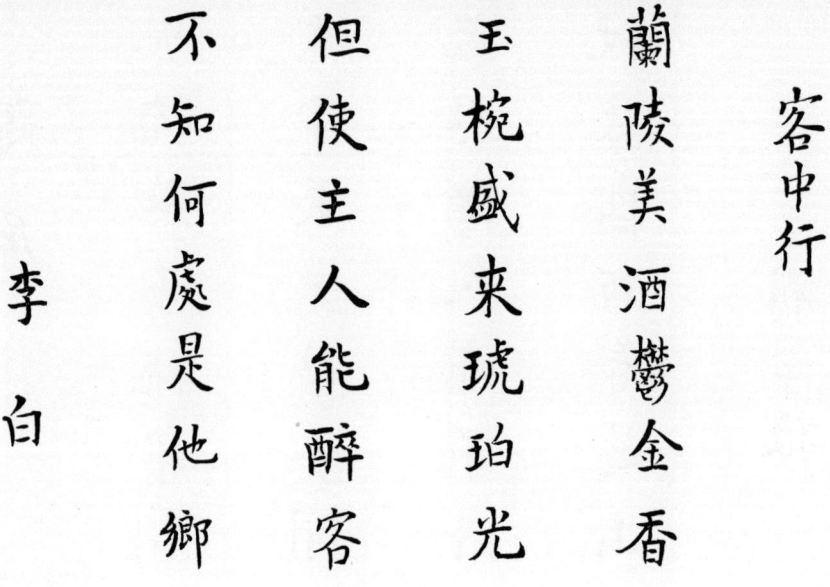

61

A TRAVELER'S SONG

How sweet the sparkling musk-root wine in Lan-ling made;
Like liquid amber how it foams in bowls of jade!
Then fill, kind host, your guests with wine to overflow,
That we may always feel at home where'er we go.

LI PO

題屏

呢喃燕子語梁間
底事來驚夢裏閒
說與傍人渾不解
杖藜攜酒看芝山

劉季孫

LINES ON A SCREEN

The twittering swallows chat about the beams,
But why must they arouse me from my dreams?
The joys I feel, though told, ah, who shall know?
With staff and wine, o'er hills of Chih I go.

LIU CHI-SUN

慢興

腸斷春江欲盡頭

杖藜徐步立芳洲

顛狂柳絮隨風舞

輕薄桃花逐水流

杜甫

63

A QUIET SCENE

I grieve to see that spring has nearly reached its end,
    With staff in hand, then slowly o'er the isle I'll roam.
Before the breeze the willow-seed plumes wildly toss,
    And peach-flowers lightly glide along the river's foam.

Tu Fu

玄都觀桃花

紫陌紅塵拂面來

無人不道看花回

玄都觀裏桃千樹

盡是劉郎去後栽

劉禹錫

THE PEACH-BLOSSOMS OF HSÜAN-TU TEMPLE

Along the purple road the noisy crowds now sway,
''We've been to see the flowers,'' one and all do say,
The thousand peach-trees which the Hsüan-tu temple grace
Have all been planted only since I left the place!

LIU YÜ-HSI

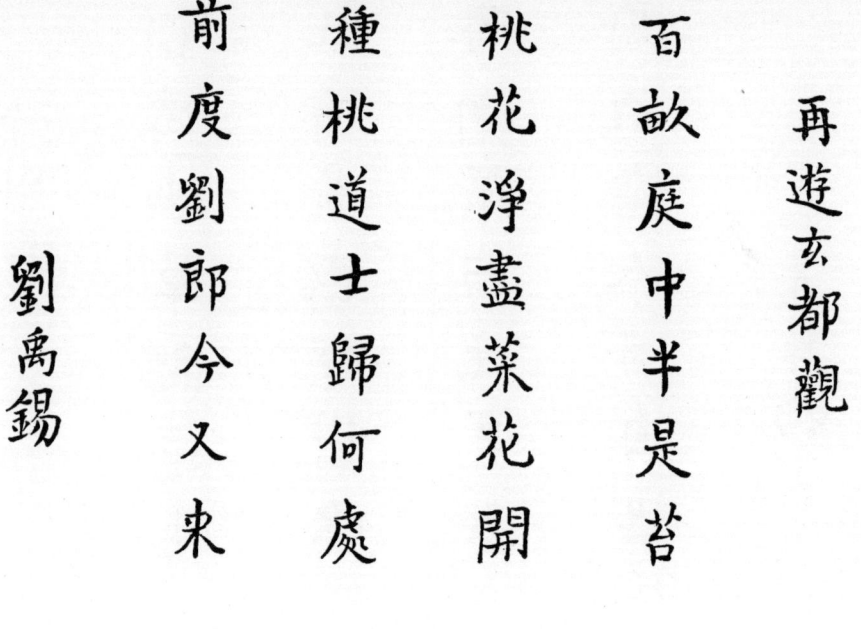

再遊玄都觀

百畝庭中半是苔
桃花淨盡菜花開
種桃道士歸何處
前度劉郎今又來

劉禹錫

65

SECOND VISIT TO THE HSÜAN-TU TEMPLE

The temple courts have turned to fields half choked with weeds;
Where once the peach-trees blossomed, flowering rape succeeds.
Whither have gone the monks who reared those peach-trees tall?
I, Mr. Liu, now come a second time to call.

LIU YÜ-HSI

滁州西澗

獨憐幽草澗邊生
上有黃鸝深樹鳴
春潮帶雨晚來急
野渡無人舟自橫

韋應物

66

A FERRY WEST OF CH'U-CHOU

I sorrow for the reeds that grow beside the stream,
Above the shady bowers yellow orioles sing.
Though swiftly flows the freshet with the vernal tides,
My ferryboat, unmanned, must idly turn and swing.

WEI YING-WU

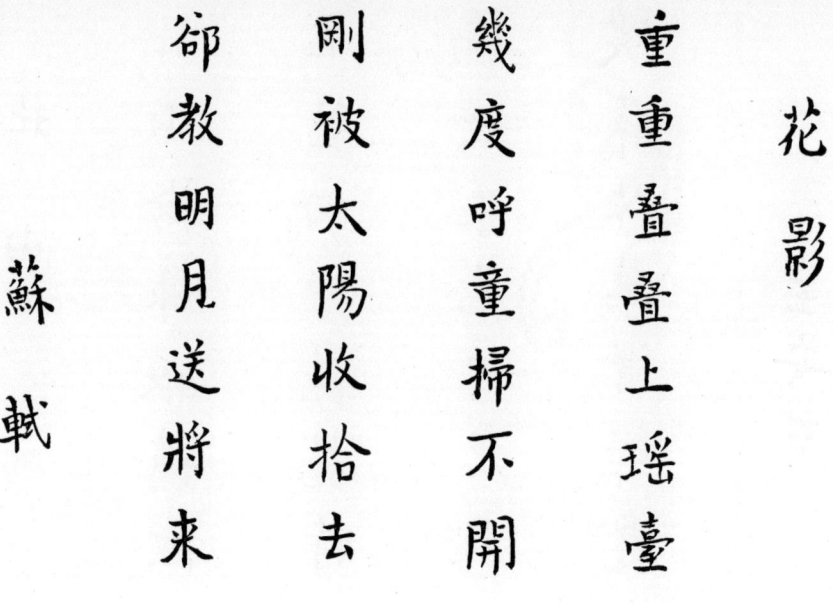

SHADOWS OF FLOWERS

The shadows up the terrace crept in thick array,
In vain the lad was told to sweep them all away.
And when the setting sun their forms withdrew,
Then lo! the silver moonlight brought them forth anew.

SU SHIH

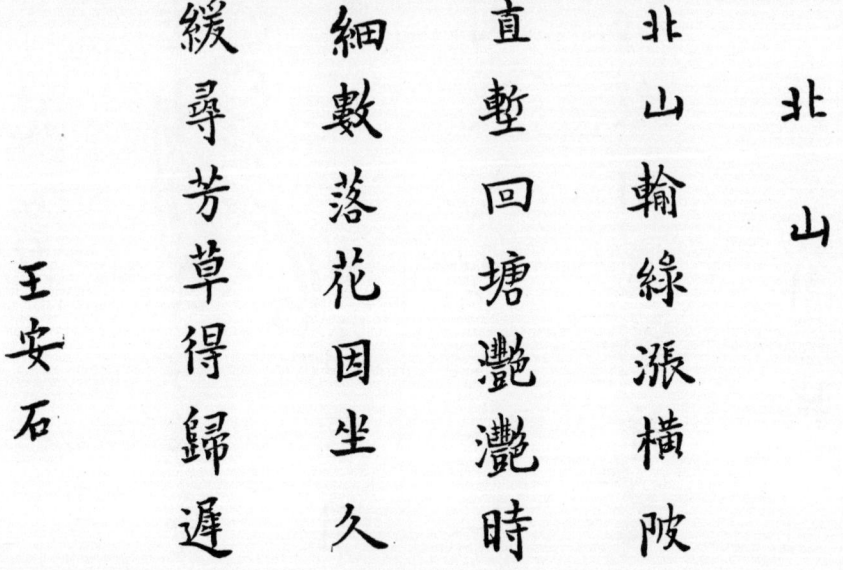

北山

北山翰綠漲橫陂
直塹回塘艷灩時
細數落花因坐久
緩尋芳草得歸遲

王安石

THE NORTHERN HILLS

The dammed-up stream was colored with the green of northern
    hills,
And all along the yawning gorges foamed the eddying rills.
Where fallen flowers engrossed my thought I there too long had
    stayed,
For searching fragrant herbs my coming home was much delayed.

WANG AN-SHIH

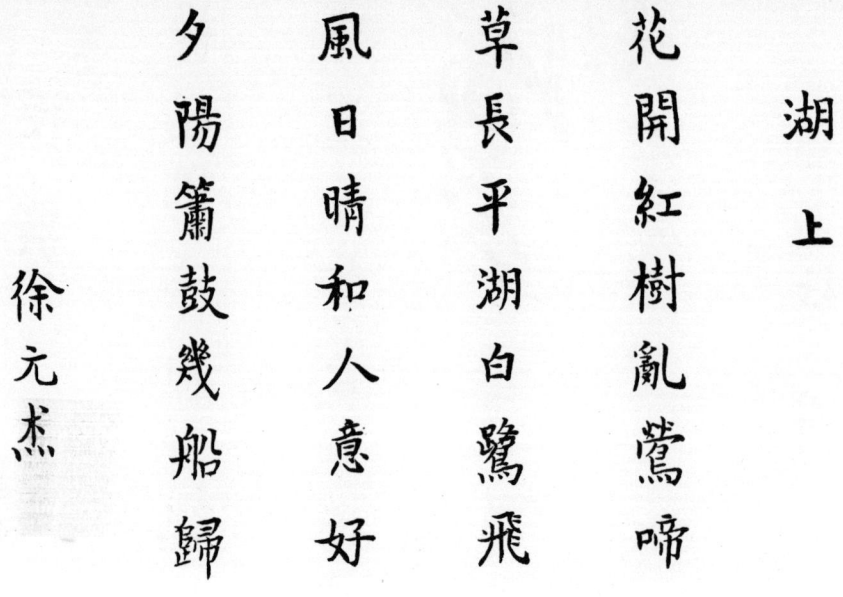

湖上

花開紅樹亂鶯啼
草長平湖白鷺飛
風日晴和人意好
夕陽簫鼓幾船歸

徐元杰

ON THE LAKE

The orioles on the flowering trees in warbling vie,
Across the sedgy lake the snow-white herons fly.
Our hearts are all attuned to such a perfect day,
At eve our boats return with music soft and gay.

HSÜ YÜAN-CHIEH

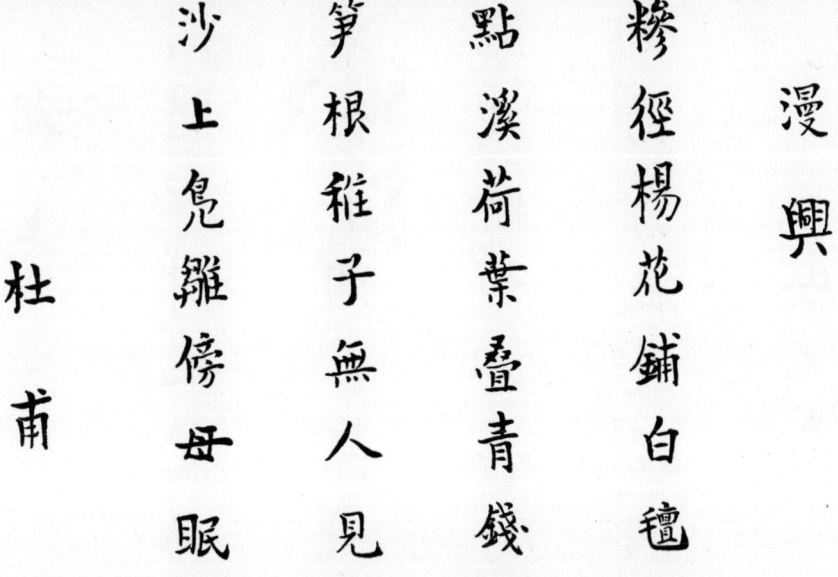

A QUIET DAY

Now whitened by willow-down, the path a long rug seems,
And thick as coins the lily-pads dot o'er the streams.
Close by the bamboo roots the unseen marmots keep,
On sandy shoal wild ducklings by their mother sleep.

TU FU

春晴

雨前初見花間蕊
雨後全無葉底花
蜂蝶紛紛過牆去
卻疑春色在隣家

王駕

A CLEAR DAY IN SPRING

Before the springtime showers only buds were seen,
When time for showers ended naught but leafy green.
Across the next wall bees and butterflies have flown,
Believing charms of spring the neighboring gardens own.

WANG CHIA

春暮

門外無人問落花
綠陰冉冉遍天涯
林鶯啼到無聲處
青草池塘獨聽蛙

曹豳

LATE SPRING

For faded flowers beyond my door none seems to care
Since folk are seeking shaded shelter everywhere.
And when the orioles' songs from woodland disappear,
The bullfrogs' croaking from their sedgy pool we'll hear.

Ts'ao Pin

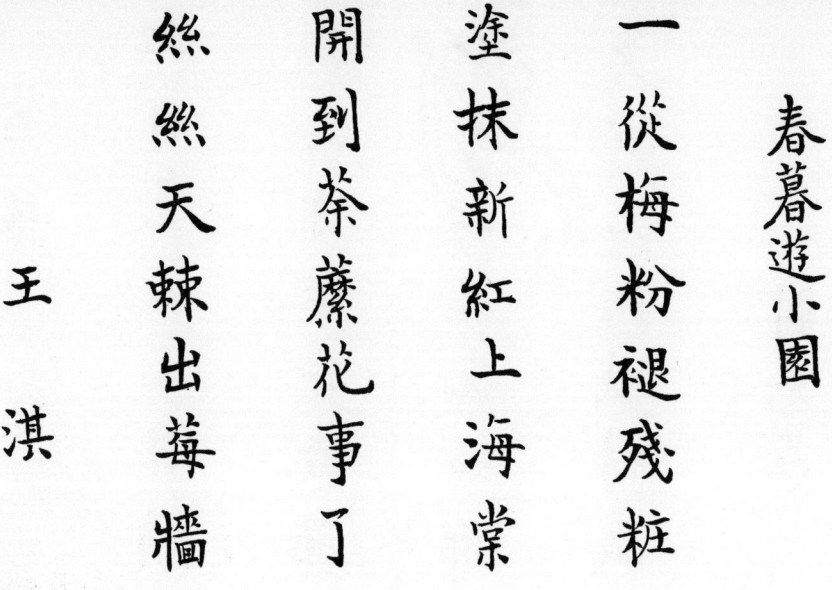

A STROLL IN THE GARDEN LATE IN SPRING

When plums begin to put their powdered dress aside,
Begonias then appear with newly painted pride.
As roses come the floral days of springtime close,
And tendrils o'er the mossy wall the bramble throws.

WANG CH'I

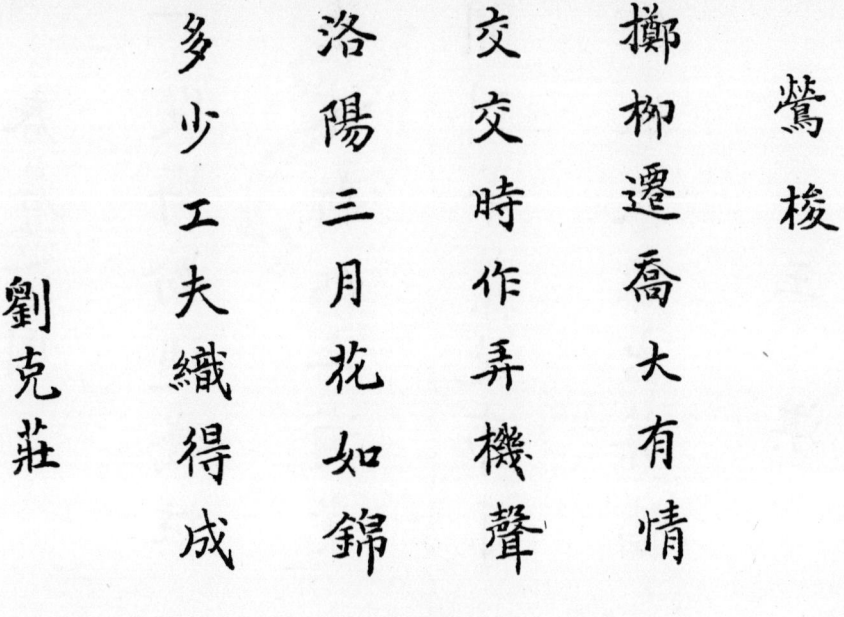

THE WEAVING ORIOLES

Now through the willows back and forth the orioles ply,
And with a click and cluck, like noisy shuttles, fly.
In Lo-yang April flowers make a field of gold,
That needs much weaving such a gorgeous work t'unfold.

LIU K'O-CHUANG

暮春即事

雙雙瓦雀行書案

點點楊花入硯池

閒坐小窗讀周易

不知春去幾多時

葉李

75

DEPARTED SPRING

From roofs the sparrows on my desk their shadows cast,
Into my inkstand willow-down was falling fast,
While I, in leisure, by the window read the *Yi*,
Nor noted when the spring had taken leave of me.

YEH LI

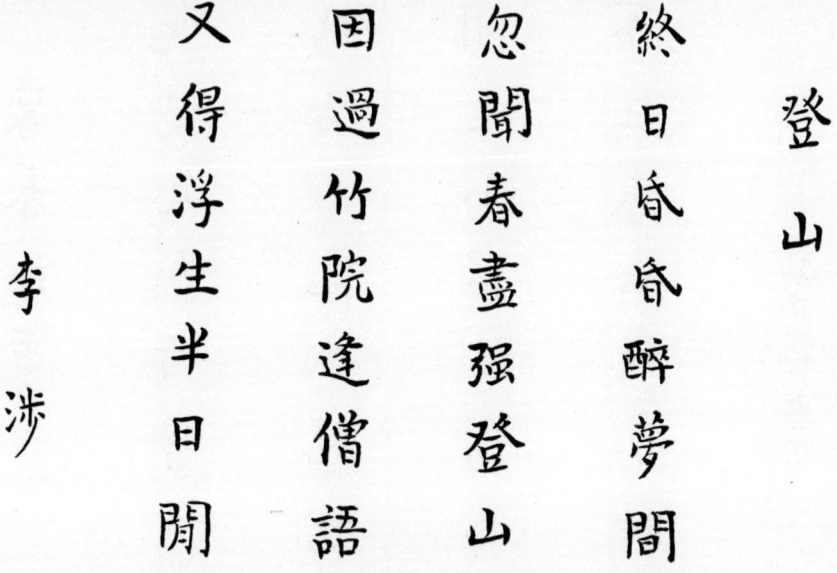

登山

終日昏昏醉夢間
忽聞春盡強登山
因過竹院逢僧語
又得浮生半日閒

李涉

76

CLIMBING THE HILLS

In drowsy state my days were passed in wine and dream,
  On hearing spring was parting, up the hill I went!
Then near a bamboo-girted temple met a priest,
  We talked for hours and one more day of leisure spent.

LI SHE

蠶婦吟

子規啼徹四更時

起視蠶稠怕葉稀

不信樓頭楊柳月

玉人歌舞未曾歸

謝枋得

77

THE COCOON-WOMAN'S SONG

The nighthawk's cry I hear and dawn is drawing nigh,
I'll see that silkworms get their leaves in full supply.
Around the house and trees the moon's about to set,
But from their dance the belles have not returned e'en yet!

HSIEH FANG-TE

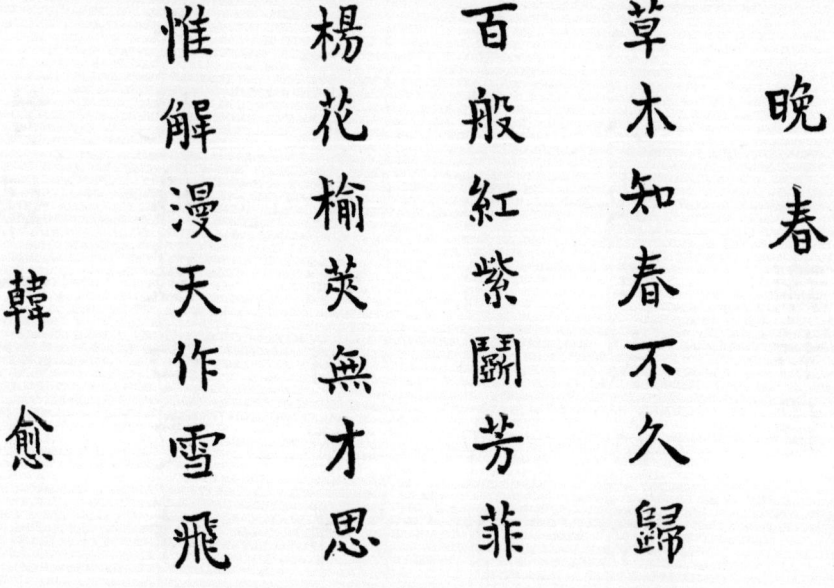

晚春

草木知春不久歸

百般紅紫鬥芳菲

楊花榆莢無才思

惟解漫天作雪飛

韓愈

END OF SPRING

The flowers know that soon must haste away the spring,
　So each in varied beauty or in sweetness vies.
But unadorned the willow-down, a thoughtless thing,
　Goes whirling through the air, and snowlike thickly flies.

HAN YÜ

傷春

準擬今春樂事濃
依然枉卻一東風
年年不帶看花眼
不是愁中即病中

楊簡

GRIEVING OVER THE PASSING OF SPRING

I thought this spring my joy would be complete;
In vain for me the east winds come and go.
No more each year the flowers my eyes will greet,
Oppressed by either sickness or by woe.

YANG CHIEN

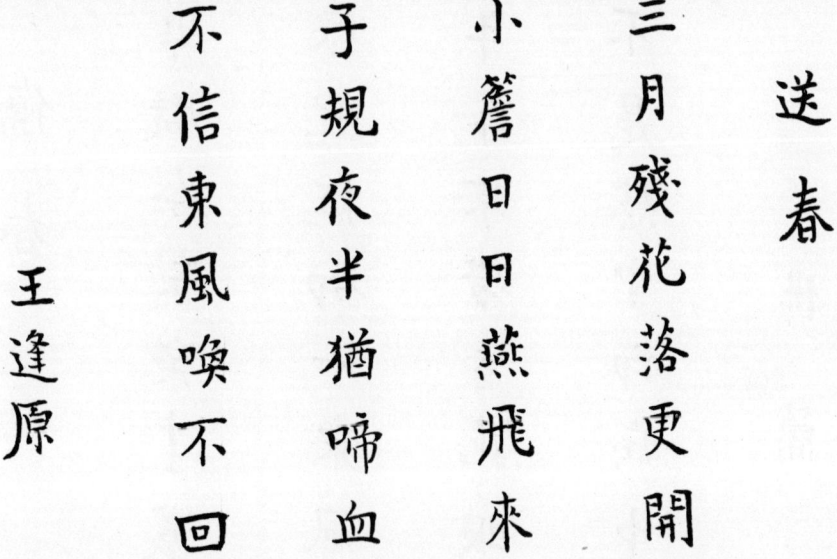

送春

三月殘花落更開
小簷日日燕飛來
子規夜半猶啼血
不信東風喚不回

王逢原

FAREWELL TO SPRING

Now April flowers bloom anew when others die.
Beneath the eaves the swallows homeward daily fly.
The nighthawk's painful cry is heard at depth of night,
Resolved on calling back the east wind from its flight.

WANG FENG-YÜAN

三月晦日送春

三月正當三十日
風光別我苦吟身
共君今夜不須睡
未到曉鐘猶是春
賈島

THE LAST EVE OF SPRING

The closing eve of spring will soon depart,
With pain its parting fills my broken heart.
O friend, we'll spend the night awake and sing,
For till the day-bell sounds, it yet is spring!

CHIA TAO

客中初夏

四月清和雨乍晴
南山當戶轉分明
更無柳絮因風起
惟有葵花向日傾

司馬光

82

BEGINNING OF SUMMER WHEN AWAY
FROM HOME

In days of May when sudden showers come and go,
The southern hills beyond in clearer outlines show.
No more the willow-plumes before the breeze disport,
But only mallows to the sun are paying court.

SSŬ-MA KWANG

有約

黃梅時節家家雨

青草池塘處處蛙

有約不來過夜半

閒敲棋子落燈花

司馬光

83

THE APPOINTED HOUR

Unceasing falls the rain when plums are growing ripe,
Within their sedgy pools the bullfrogs croak and pipe.
The hour they named has passed, my friends have failed to call,
A careless tap with chessman makes the lamp-wick fall.

SSŬ-MA KWANG

初夏睡起

梅子流酸濺齒牙

芭蕉分綠上窗紗

日長睡起無情思

閒看兒童捉柳花

楊簡

84

RISING FROM A SUMMER NAP

Juicy plums so tart; my teeth feel keen.
Plantain leaves on gauze reflect their green.
Rising from my nap in summer days,
I watch the children willow-seed plumes chase.

YANG CHIEN

三衢道中

梅子黄時日日晴

小溪汎盡卻山行

綠陰不減来時路

添得黄鸝四五聲

曾紆

85

ON THE CH'U-CHOU ROAD

When plums are ripe, then fair's the weather every day.
We follow up some stream or climb among the hills.
As green as when we came are shades along the way,
But now I hear the flaming orioles' tuneful trills.

TSENG YÜ

即景

竹搖清影罩幽窗
兩兩時禽噪夕陽
謝卻海棠飛盡絮
困人天氣日初長

朱淑貞

THE PASSING MOMENT

Their shadows 'gainst my window waving bamboos throw,
The mated songsters chatter in the sunset glow.
Crabapples now are past, and willow-plumes away,
To me the longer seems each languid summer day.

CHU SHU-CHENG

夏日

乳鴨池塘水淺深
熟梅天氣半晴陰
東園載酒西園醉
摘盡枇杷一樹金

戴復古

A SUMMER DAY

In deep or shallow pools the ducklings dive away,
The plums are ripe and clouds or sunshine claim the day.
In gardens east and west our wine by turns we sip,
The golden *P'i-p'a* fruit from laden branches strip.

TAI FU-KU

晚樓閒望

四顧山光接水光

凭欄十里芰荷香

清風明月無人管

并作南來一味涼

王安石

88

EVENING SCENE FROM A BALCONY

On every side the tints of hill and water blend,
Their perfume to my balcony distant lilies send.
Unheeded are the soft, pure breeze and moonbeams bright,
Both coming from the south, how cool they make the night!

WANG AN-SHIH

山居夏日

綠樹陰濃夏日長
樓臺倒影入池塘
水晶簾動微風起
滿架薔薇一院香

高駢

89

SUMMER IN A MOUNTAIN RETREAT

The shade of trees is deep and long the summer days,
Reflected towers on every lakelet I can trace,
Like crystal curtains in the breeze the ripples bend,
And trellised roses through the garden perfumes send.

KAO P'IEN

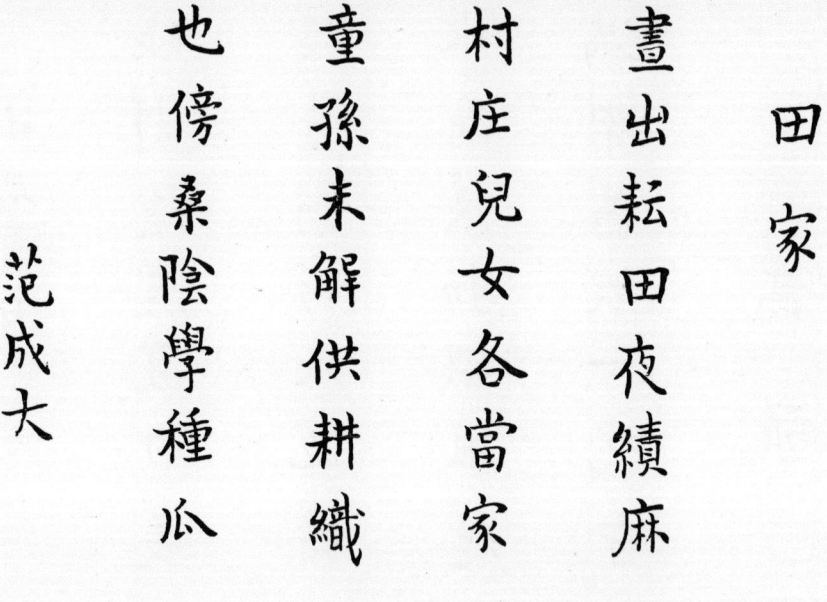

田家

畫出耘田夜績麻
村庄兒女各當家
童孫未解供耕織
也傍桑陰學種瓜

范成大

A FARMER'S HOME

They tilled the fields at dawn, they spun the hemp at eve,
Thus o'er their toils the rural swains and matrons pored.
Their children, all too young to learn to plow or weave,
Beneath the mulberry shade would play at planting gourd.

FAN CH'ENG-TA

村庄即事

綠遍山原白滿川
子規聲裏雨如烟
鄉村四月閒人少
繞了蠶桑又插田

范成大

A RURAL SCENE

The streams are foaming white; fields bright with green,
Amid misty rain the nighthawk's cry is keen.
Among farms in May no leisure hands are found,
When silk time ends, then planting rice comes around.

FAN CH'ENG-TA

題榴花

五月榴花照眼明
枝間時見子初成
可憐此地無車馬
顛倒蒼苔落絳英

朱熹

LINES TO THE POMEGRANATE FLOWERS

In June the pomegranates' blooms are dazzling bright,
Their tender fruits on branches lure our sight.
What pity here no carriage more shall pass,
Ere such bright flowers fade upon the grass.

CHU HSI

茅簷

茅簷常掃淨無苔
花木成蹊手自栽
一水護田將綠遶
兩山排闥送青來

王安石

93

THE THATCHED EAVES

Beneath the eaves the weeds are swept away with care,
The flowering shrubs I reared have formed a pathway fair.
The stream that feeds the fields through endless verdure wends,
Each hill beyond to me its wealth of emerald sends.

WANG AN-SHIH

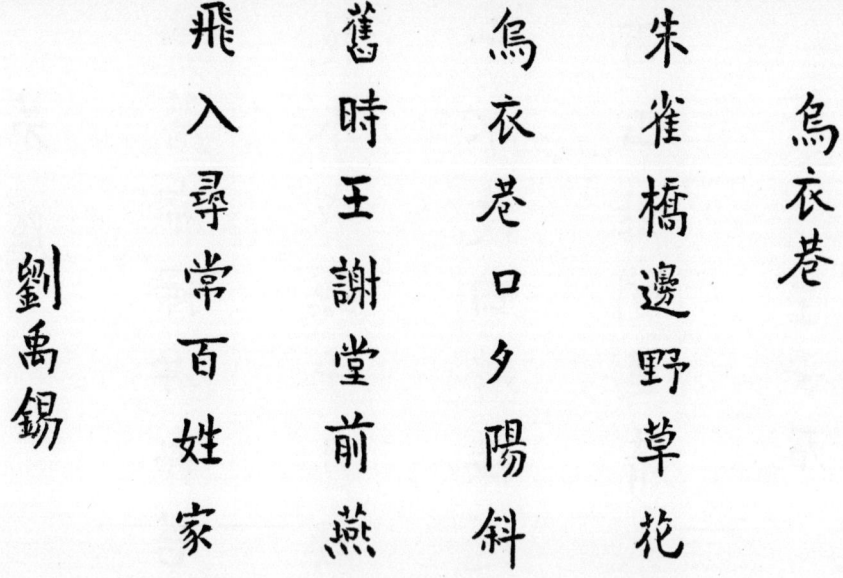

WU-YI OR SWALLOWS' LANE

Beside the Chu-chiao Bridge wildflowers thickly grow,
Along the Wu-yi Lane the sun is setting low.
Where once the swallows knew the mansions of the great,
They now to humbler homes would fly to nest and mate.

LIU YÜ-HSI

送使安西

渭城朝雨浥輕塵
客舍青青柳色新
勸君更盡一杯酒
西出陽關無故人

王維

95

FAREWELL TO AN ENVOY ON HIS MISSION TO KUCHA

The morning rain has washed the Wei-ch'eng dust away,
The willows 'round the inn their fresh green robes display.
I urge thee, friend, another cup of wine to drain,
Since west of Yang-kwan Pass you'll seek for friends in vain.

WANG WEI

題北榭碑

一為遷客去長沙

西望長安不見家

黃鶴樓中吹玉笛

江城五月落梅花

李白

LINES ON A MEMORIAL TABLET

An exile now I go to Ch'ang-sha far away,
But westward toward Ch'ang-an my eyes still homeward stray.
On Yellow-Crane Tower, with my flute, I'll play the tune
Of "Fallen Plum-flowers," thus, to cheer this town in June.

Li Po

題淮南寺

南去北來休便休

白蘋吹盡楚江秋

道人不是悲秋客

一任晚山相對愁

程顥

97

LINES WRITTEN IN HWAI-NAN TEMPLE

I wander north and south and rest me here and there,
The stream is white with flowers, the landscape now is bare.
I come not here to mourn the work of autumn breeze,
The hills on either bank may mourn if they so please.

CH'ENG HAO

秋月

清溪流過碧山頭
空水澄鮮一色秋
隔斷紅塵三十里
白雲紅葉兩悠悠

程顥

AUTUMN

Close by the emerald hills there flows the crystal stream,
Transparent pools with richest tints of autumn gleam,
Far from the wrangling world this scene doth softly rest,
By fleecy clouds and purple leaves profusely dressed.

CH'ENG HAO

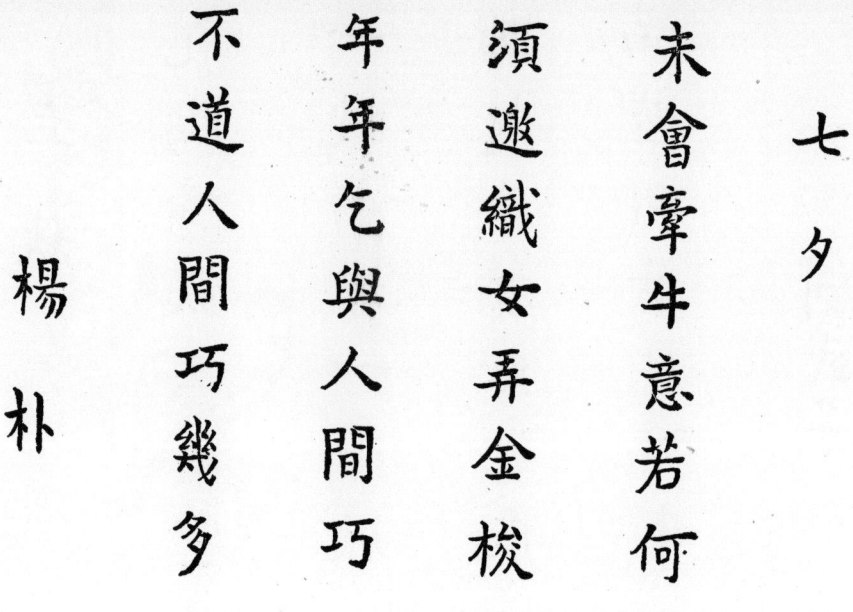

七夕

未會牽牛意若何
須邀織女弄金梭
年年乞與人間巧
不道人間巧幾多

楊朴

99

EVENING OF THE SEVENTH DAY
OF THE SEVENTH MONTH

What shall we do ere Herdboy and Weaver meet?
To work her shuttle we will beg the Weaver sweet.
Fair maidens yearly ask the Weaver teach them skill,
But just how much they learn remains a secret still.

YANG P'O

立秋

乳鴉啼散玉屏空
一枕新涼一扇風
睡起秋聲無覓處
滿堦桐葉月明中

劉武子

100

BEGINNING OF AUTUMN

The cawing rooks are gone, the leafy screen is bare,
Across my pillow come cool draughts of evening air.
The voice of autumn wakes me, though the autumn's fled;
With *Wu-t'ung* leaves the moonlit steps are thickly spread.

LIU WU-TZŬ

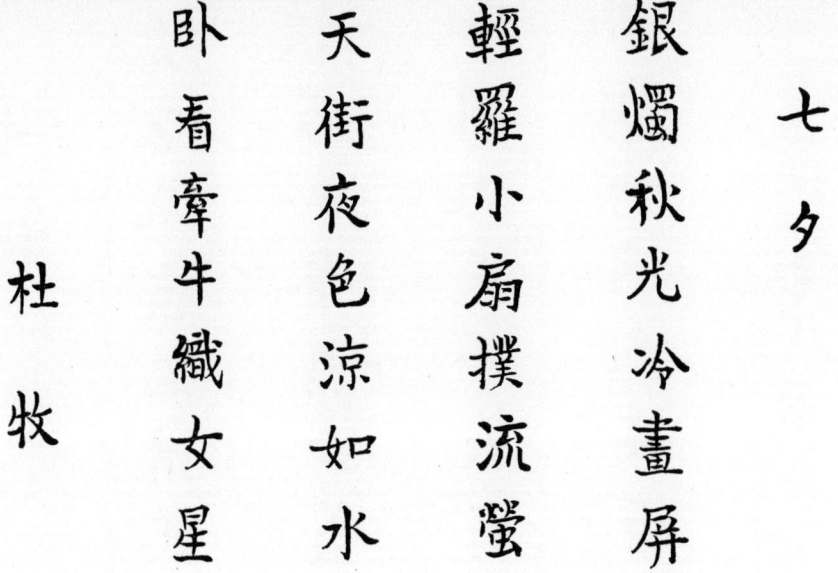

AN AUTUMN EVE

Against the painted screen the moon projects its light,
    With silken fan the flitting glowworms I evade.
Upon the garden roof, where cool as liquid seems the night,
    I lie and watch the Herdboy and his Weaving-Maid.

Tu Mu

中秋

暮雲收盡溢清寒
銀漢無聲轉玉盤
此生此夜不長好
明月明年何處看

杜牧

102

MID-AUTUMN

The evening clouds are gone, the air is cool and clear,
The Milky Way is mute, the moon a shining sphere.
This life and lovely night will not last long for me,
Then where shall I another year this bright moon see?

Tu Mu

江樓有感

獨上江樓思悄然
月光如水水如天
同來玩月人何在
風景依稀似去年

趙嘏

103

SADNESS ON ASCENDING A TOWER
BY THE RIVER BANK

The tower by the stream I mount alone and sigh,
How softly blends the light of moon and stream and sky!
Where now those who enjoyed the moon with me? No more!
But quite the same the landscape seems as days of yore.

CHAO CHIA

西湖

山外青山樓外樓
西湖歌舞幾時休
暖風薰得遊人醉
直把杭州作汴州

林淇

104

THE WEST LAKE

Peaks rise beyond the peaks, while towers on towers crowd.
The song and dance proceed on West Lake long and loud.
The soft and drowsy breeze the wandering throng enchants.
Hang-chow, the new-found home, their old Pien-chow supplants.

LIN CH'I

西湖

畢竟西湖六月中
風光不與四時同
接天蓮葉無窮碧
映日荷花別樣紅

蘇軾

105

A WEST LAKE VIEW IN JULY

Ah, truly, on the Western Lake in summer days,
Are scenes surpassing all the other months' displays.
Now endless verdure of the lotus meets the sky,
And sparkling lilies, too, assume a redder dye.

Su Shih

湖上初雨

水光瀲灩晴偏好

山色空濛雨亦奇

欲把西湖比西子

淡粧濃抹也相宜

蘇軾

106

RAIN ON THE WEST LAKE

The lake first sparkled in the sun's bright dazzling sheen,
Then wonder-working showers the verdant hills would screen.
For varied charms the West Lake well may I compare
To Hsi-Tzŭ, who, adorned or not, alike was fair.

SU SHIH

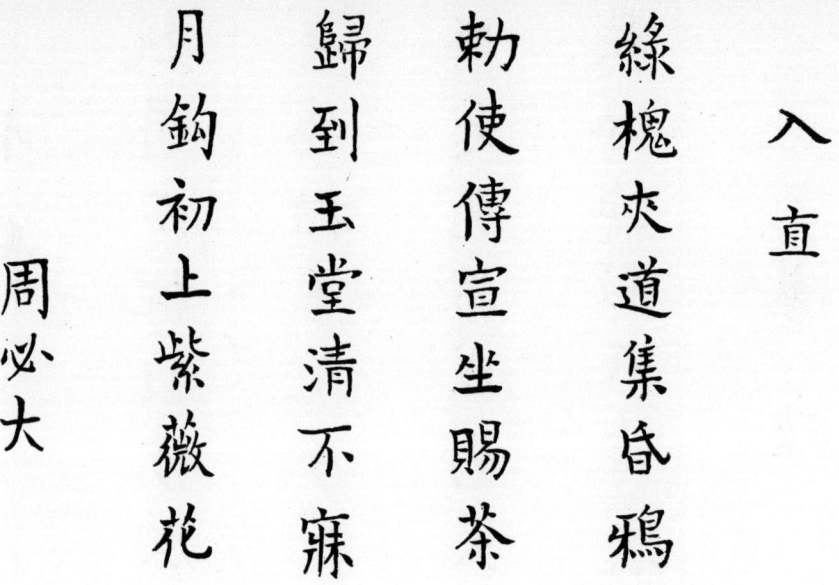

入直

綠槐夾道集昏鴉
勅使傳宣坐賜茶
歸到玉堂清不寐
月鈎初上紫薇花

周必大

107

ON DUTY AT COURT

The crows were perched on locust trees along the court.
When summoned to the Presence, seat and tea were brought.
Though back to Jewel Hall I went, I never slept,
For up the myrtle-flowers the crescent moonbeams crept.

CHOU PI-TA

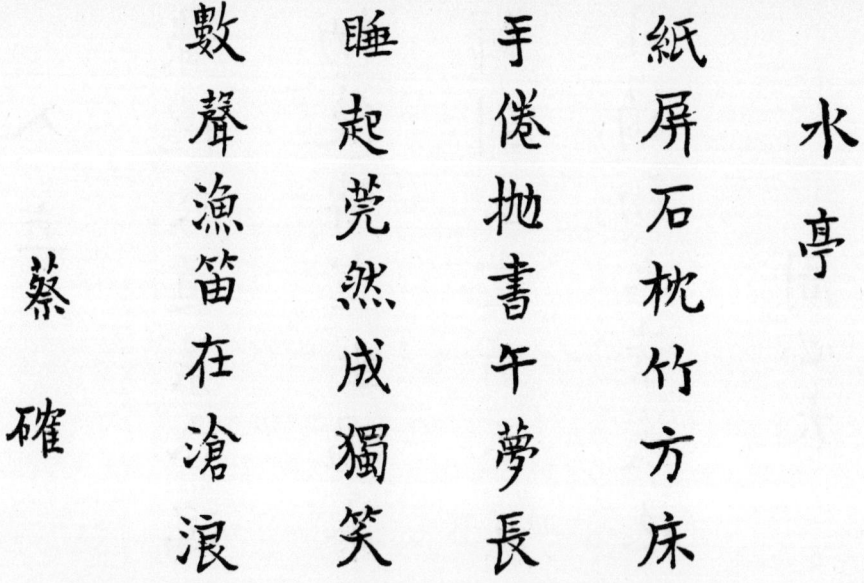

水亭

紙屏石枕竹方床
于倦抛書午夢長
睡起莞然成獨笑
數聲漁笛在滄浪

蔡確

108

A PAVILION BY THE WATER

Well screened on bamboo couch, and pillowed on a stone,
  I doze at noon, the volume fallen by my side.
And when I wake, o'er queerest dreams I laugh alone,
  And hear the fisher's flute along the rippling tide.

Ts'ai Ch'io

禁鎖

禁門深鎖寂無譁
濃墨淋漓兩相麻
唱徹五更天未曉
一墀月浸紫薇花

洪遵

109

IN THE FORBIDDEN COURT

The court was guarded well, no sound disturbed my ears.
　The royal edict soon I penned with flowing ink.
The last watch then was called before the dawn appeared,
　I saw the moon behind the myrtles slowly sink.

HUNG TSUN

觀書有感

半畝方塘一鑑開

天光雲影共徘徊

問渠那得清如許

為有源頭活水來

朱熹

REFLECTION AFTER READING

My little lake was like a mirror spread,
Across its surface lights and shadows sped.
"Whence came this limpidness of thine?" I said.
It answered: "From a living fountainhead."

CHU HSI

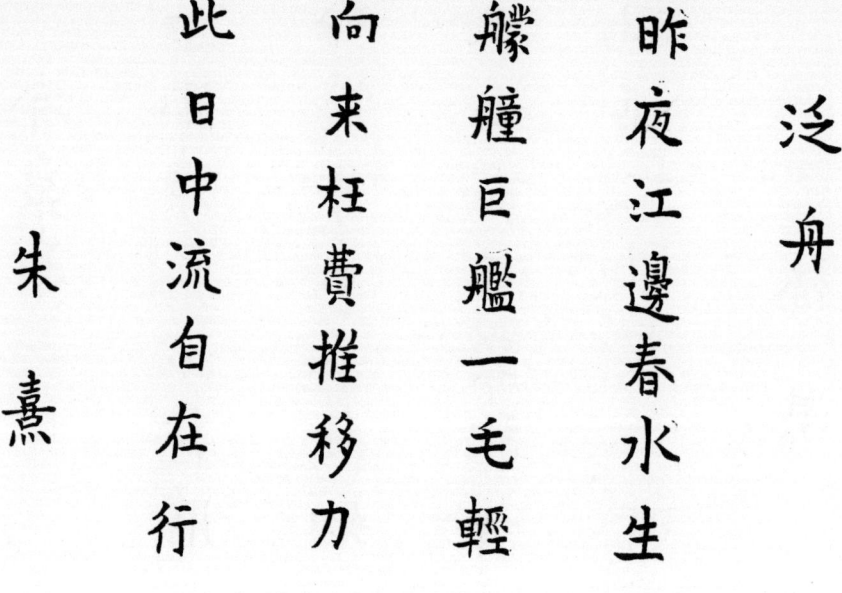

泛舟

昨夜江邊春水生
艨艟巨艦一毛輕
向来枉費推移力
此日中流自在行

朱熹

THE FLOATED SHIP

The freshets of the spring o'erswelled the banks last night,
The mighty ship is floating like a feather—light.
Ere this, with every effort vain, we pushed and pried,
But now, adown midstream, we see her freely glide.

CHU HSI

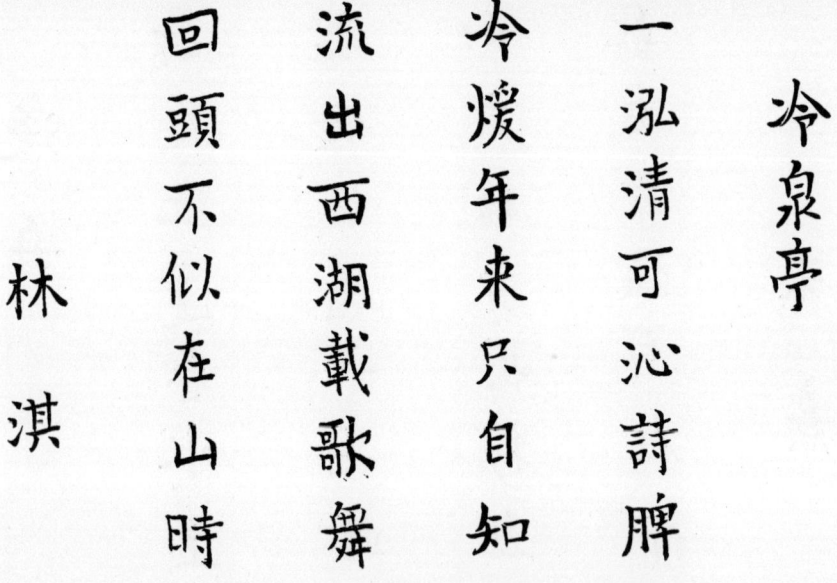

冷泉亭

一泓清可沁詩脾
冷煖年来只自知
流出西湖載歌舞
回頭不似在山時

林淇

112

TO THE MOUNTAIN BROOK

O Brook, thy crystal stream can cleanse a poet's heart.
Alone thou feel'st the heat and cold the years impart.
But once in song and dance thou join'st on Western Lake,
Then lo, thy mountain purity will thee forsake!

LIN CH'I

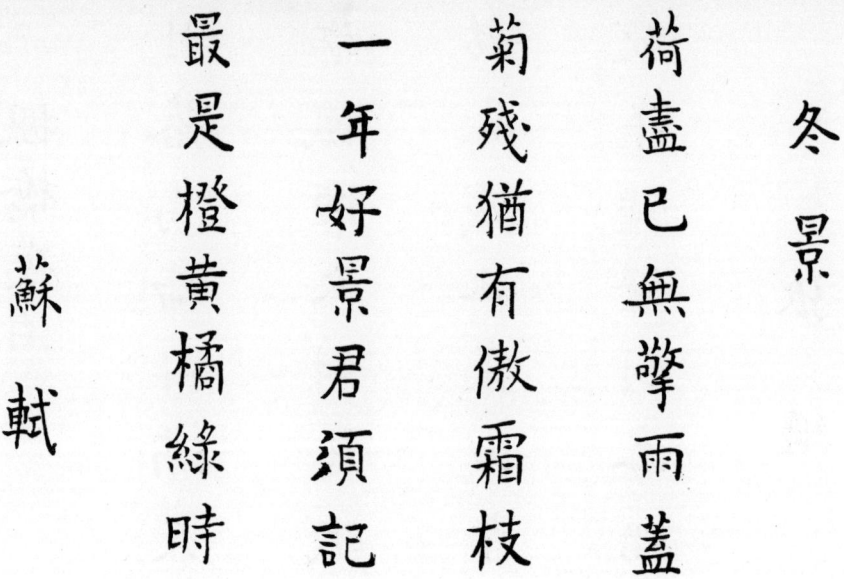

冬景

荷盡已無擎雨蓋
菊殘猶有傲霜枝
一年好景君須記
最是橙黃橘綠時

蘇軾

A WINTER SCENE

No more the lotus-leaves that hold the rain appear,
Though yet chrysanthemums their frosted stalks would rear.
O friend, bear well in mind, the year's best sights are seen,
When oranges their golden yellow mix with green.

SU SHIH

楓橋夜泊

月落烏啼霜滿天
江楓漁火對愁眠
姑蘇城外寒山寺
夜半鐘聲到客船

張繼

ANCHORED AT NIGHT BY THE MAPLE BRIDGE

The moon is setting, rooks disturb the frosty air,
I watch by mapled banks the fishing-torches flare.
Outside the Suchow walls, from Han-shan Temple's bell,
I hear its sound aboard and feel its midnight spell.

CHANG CHI

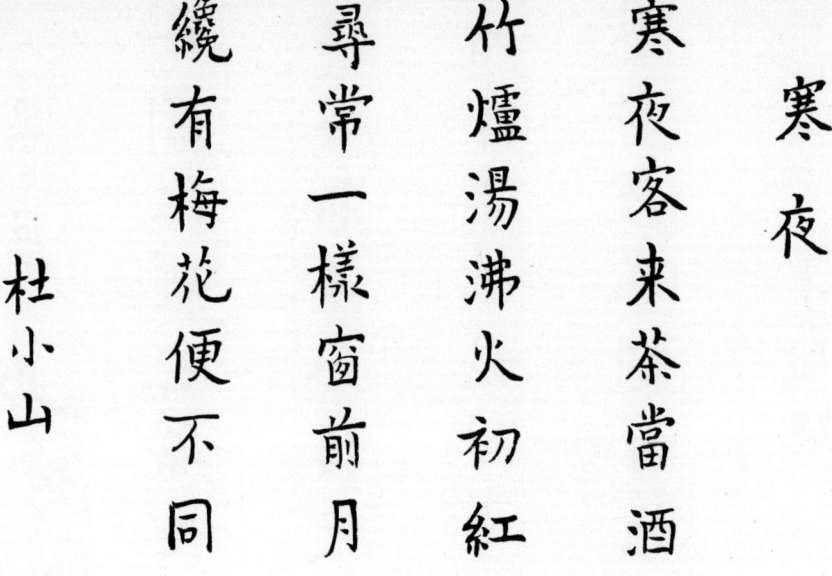

A COLD NIGHT

The night is cold, not wine, but tea my guest I'll bring.
The kettle on the glowing fire is simmering.
Outside the window sheds the moon her welcome light,
But with some prunus blossoms what a charm has night!

TU HSIAO-SHAN

霜月

初聞征雁已無蟬
百尺樓臺水接天
青女素娥俱耐冷
月中霜裏鬥嬋娟

李商隱

116

THE TWO FAIRIES

When wild geese first I hear, cicadas then retreat;
From lofty tower I see where sky and water meet.
The Tender-Maid and Lady-Fair the cold defy—
In frost and moon they reign, in beauty ever vie.

LI SHANG-YIN

梅

不受塵埃半點侵
竹籬茅舍自甘心
只因誤識林和靖
惹得詩人說到今

王淇

117

THE PLUM-TREES' COMPLAINT

We ne'er allowed a speck of dust to soil our flowers,
Content to grow beside the humble cottage bowers.
But since that songster Lin Ho-ching we've come to know,
We have from him of song an endless flow.

WANG CHI

早春

南枝繞放兩三柁

雪裏吟香弄粉些

淡淡著烟濃著月

深深籠水淺籠沙

白玉蟾

118

EARLY SPRING

The branches facing south have just begun to bloom,
Amid the snow I sing of flowers with mild perfume.
How light the hanging mist, how bright the moon now seems,
One shines on sandy shoals, one thickly veils the streams.

PAI YÜ-CH'AN

雪梅

梅雪爭春未肯降

騷人閣筆費評章

梅須遜雪三分白

雪卻輸梅一段香

盧梅坡

119

THE SNOW AND PLUM-FLOWERS' RIVALRY

Plum and snow in beauty oft have vied.
A pen is stayed; the bard can scarce decide.
In whiteness flow'rs to flakes three parts must yield;
In sweetness flakes to flow'rs must grant the field.

LU MEI-PO

雪梅

有梅無雪不精神
有雪無詩俗了人
日暮詩成天又雪
與梅并作十分春

盧梅坡

THE SNOW AND PLUM-FLOWERS

How impotent are flow'rs without the snow!
And without verse how vain the human show!
At eve with falling snow and poetry
And flowers, spring is a perfect trilogy.

LU MEI-PO

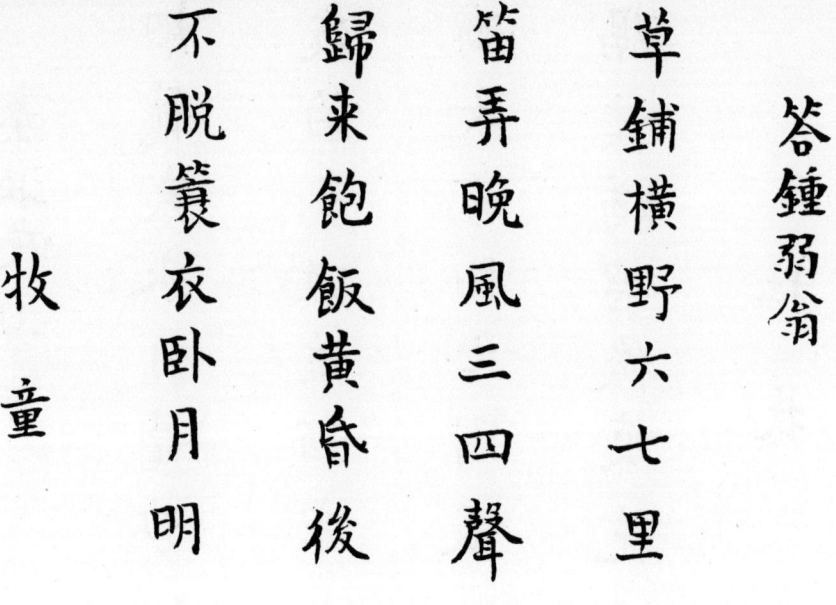

REPLY TO CHUNG JO-WENG

I roam the grassy fields that stretch away for miles,
My flute with dulcet notes the breezy eve beguiles.
When back at dusk my frugal meal I finish soon,
I sleep, with palm-leaf coat still on, beneath the moon.

HERDBOY (MU T'UNG)

秦淮夜泊

烟籠寒水月籠沙
夜泊秦淮近酒家
商女不知亡國恨
隔溪猶唱後庭花

杜牧

122

ANCHORED AT NIGHT IN THE CH'IN-HWAI DISTRICT (NANKING)

The mist the river veils, the moon shines on the sand,
We're moored tonight in Ch'in-hwai where the wineshops stand.
The song-girls here know not of kingdoms' dying pains,
So drifting o'er the stream come Hou-t'ing-hua's sad strains.

TU MU

NOTES TO POEMS

Poem No. 1.—The third line also means political changes, veiled under the change of weather. The fourth line suggests that many officials were cashiered, degraded, transferred to distant regions, or removed, under such political changes.

Quite a number of poems in this collection have a double meaning or undercurrent of thought. It was safer for poets of the old days to say things in metaphor than in direct statement. Contemporaneous subjects are treated in a historical sense to avoid trouble. This is the reason why incidents in the T'ang and Sung periods were compared to historical facts in the Han dynasty or earlier periods. A double meaning in poetry is not confined to the Chinese. If we search for it we will notice it in the works of Longfellow, Tennyson, and others too numerous to mention.

Lines couched in double meaning are found in poems Nos. 1, 9, 43, 58, 65, 66, 67, 79, 110, 111, 112, notes to which appear in their consecutive order.

Poem No. 2.—Lo-yang 洛陽 was the eastern capital of the T'ang dynasty. It is the present Honan prefecture in the northwestern part of Honan province.

Chiang-ling 江嶺, also known as Yü-ling 庾嶺, the chain of mountains separating Kiang-si 江西 province from Chekiang 浙江 and Fukien 福建 provinces.

Poem No. 3.—Hwai River 淮水, rising in the southern part of Honan 河南 province, flowing through the northern part of Anhui 安徽 province, empties into the Hung-tse Lake 洪澤湖, in northern Kiangsu 江蘇 province and debouches into the Yellow Sea 黃海.

Poem No. 4.—Lo-yang 洛陽 (see note to poem No. 2).

Wu-ling 五陵, the residential quarters of the nobles and high officials at Ch'ang-an 長安, the western capital of the T'ang 唐 dynasty. Ch'ang-an is now known as Hsi-an 西安, in central Shen-si 陝西 province.

Poem No. 5.—Ching-t'ing Hills 敬亭山, in the northern part of Hsüanch'eng 宣城, district in the prefecture of Ning-kuo 寧國府, in the southeastern part of An-hui 安徽 province.

·123·

Poem No. 6.—Heron Pagoda 鸛 鵲 樓 is in P'u-chou 蒲 州, in the south-western corner of Shan-si 山 西 province, on the Yellow River 黃 河.

Poem No. 7.—Princess Yung-lo 永 樂 公 主.

Since the Han 漢 dynasty, 206 B.C.–A.D. 220, and through the T'ang 唐 and subsequent dynasties, it was sometimes necessary for the Chinese emperors, for political reasons, to give a princess in marriage to some powerful Khan of the northern tribes in order to secure his allegiance and keep the northern borders from raids and incursions. This poem refers to just such an event. The princess is generally not a daughter of the emperor but the daughter of an imperial clansman, having the title of "princess" conferred on her when she is selected as the bride of a Khan or chieftain.

Poem No. 8.—Yi-chou 伊 州, also known as Yi-wu 伊 吾, was the ancient name of the present district round Hami 哈 密 in Chinese Turkestan.

Liao-hsi 遼 西, west of the Liao River, in the province of Feng-t'ien 奉 天, or Sheng-king 盛 京, now renamed Liao Ning 遼 寧, the most southerly of the three eastern provinces forming Manchuria.

Poem No. 9.—The third line also means that the imperial favor is never certain, as varying as the winds of the spring, and many are the rivals at court, with cunning schemes to supplant a good man, but a loyal minister should be guided by loyalty alone and serve the emperor in a straightforward course. *Yüch'ieh* 玉 階 is jade or marble steps—meant for the emperor, as "the throne" is used for the sovereign—a metonymy.

Poem No. 12.—趙 氏 連 城 璧, "the gem of Chao worth many cities." This allusion refers to Prince Chao 昭 王 of the state of Ch'in 秦, who wished to give up fifteen cities in exchange for the gem possessed by the state of Chao 趙. Lin Siang-ju 藺 相 如, an officer of Chao, was intrusted with the gem to go to Ch'in, but on his arrival he found the Prince of Ch'in had no intention of giving up the cities. Lin then said to the Prince, "Since your highness will not hand over the cities, your humble servant will return the gem to Chao." This event took place in 345 B.C. (see notes to poems Nos. 16 and 18).

Poem No. 14.—Ch'in 秦, an ancient feudal state, the modern Shen-si 陝 西 (see notes to poems Nos. 4 and 12).

Wu-ling 五 陵 (see note to poem No. 4).

Poem No. 15.—Heng-t'ang 橫 塘, a district in Nanking, outside the Ch'i-lin Gate 麒 麟 門.

·124·

Poem No. 16.—Fan Shu 范叔, or Fan Ch'u 范雎. The state of Wei, one of the small feudal states, 403–241 B.C., southern part of present Shan-si 山西 and northern portion of Honan 河南, sent two ambassadors to the state of Ch'i 齊, the present Shantung. They were Hsü Ku 須賈, the senior, and Fan Ch'u, 范雎, the junior member of the mission. The Prince of Ch'i took a great liking to Fan and sent him presents of beef and wine. When the embassy returned to Wei, Hsü Ku reported that Fan had accepted presents. The prime minister, Wei Chi, suspecting that Fan was bribed for divulging state secrets, had him punished so severely that a rib was broken and some teeth knocked out. Fan pretended death, was thrown into the gutter, and thus escaped. He entered the state of Ch'in and changed his name to Chang Lu 張祿. Eventually he obtained an audience with Prince Chao of Ch'in and later was made prime minister.

When Hsü Ku was sent on a mission to Ch'in, Fan, dressed in shabby clothes, made a private call on Hsü Ku at the latter's residence. On seeing Fan in such a wretched condition, Hsü Ku was greatly surprised and said, "Is my friend still enjoying good health?" He also asked Fan to stay to dinner and remarked, "I never knew that you had been reduced to this pitiable condition." Thereupon Hsü took off his own robe and put it on Fan.

When Fan returned to his own mansion, he drove a big chariot drawn by four horses, acting as the charioteer, and conveyed Hsü Ku to the official mansion of the prime minister of Ch'in on his official call. Fan entered the mansion while Hsü waited outside ready for an announcement to be received.

After waiting a long time Hsü ventured to ask the doorkeeper what kept the charioteer so long. The doorkeeper said, "He is the prime minister." On hearing this Hsü Ku shook with fear. When presented to Fan Shu he knelt down and begged for mercy, saying, "I never realized that you had risen to such eminence." Fan replied, "You are not dead today because you still can show pity by clothing me with your robe. For this act I forgive the wrong you have done me."

Poem No. 18.—Yen and Chao 燕趙, two powerful feudal states, Yen in modern Chili province, altered to Ho-pei recently, and Chao in modern Shan-si. The feudal period in China was about 600–200 B.C. (for Chao see notes to poem No. 12).

Poem No. 19.—K'wang-lu 匡廬, or Lu-shan 廬山 Mountains, near Kiu-kiang in Kiang-si province. The foreign sanitarium of Ku-ling is in the Lu-shan Range.

·125·

Six Dynasties 六朝, here translated "realms forgotten," were six short-lived dynasties reigning independently in different parts of China. They were: Sung 宋, A.D. 420–79; Ch'i 齊, A.D. 479–502; Liang 梁, A.D. 502–57; Ch'en 陳, A.D. 557–89; Northern Wei 北魏, A.D. 386–535; Northern Chou 北周, A.D. 557–89. These were finally absorbed by the Sui 隨 dynasty, A.D. 589–618.

Poem No. 20.—*Yi* or *Yi Ching* 易經, the "Book of Changes," the oldest classic in China, compiled in the Chou 周 dynasty, 1122–255 B.C.

Ch'u 楚, an ancient feudal state, including parts of modern Hunan and Hupei provinces (see note to poem No. 18).

Poem No. 24.—Wu-hu 五湖, also known as T'ai-hu 太湖, a large lake west of Suchow in Kiangsu province.

Ancient events 千古事 refer to the history of the feudal state of Wu 吳, modern Kiangsu, and Yüeh 越, modern Chekiang, capital in K'uei-chi 會稽. Wu first conquered Yüeh but was in turn annihilated by the latter. (For feudal period see note to poem No. 18.)

Poem No. 27.—Fen 汾 River flows through Shansi and empties into the Yellow River.

Poem No. 28.—Shu 蜀, the ancient name of the province of Sze-ch'uan 四川. Lo-yang 洛陽 (see notes to poems Nos. 2 and 4).

Poem No. 31.—Han 漢 dynasty, 206 B.C.—A.D. 220.

"The Noble Steed," or "the Noble Censor" who rode on a piebald horse, an appellation given to Huan Tien 桓典 of the Eastern Han dynasty, A.D. 25–220. He was a bold and upright censor under the Emperor Ling. Huan Tien died A.D. 201 (Giles).

Poem No. 32.—Wu-ling 武陵, an ancient name for Ch'ang-te 常德, prefecture in the northern part of Hunan province and west of the Tung-t'ing Lake 洞庭湖.

Ta-liang 大梁, another name for the state of Wei 魏, a feudal state (see note to poem No. 16).

Hsin-ling 信陵, or Prince Wu-chi 無忌 of Wei 魏, third century B.C. He was a liberal and generous prince and attracted to him many men of talent.

Poem No. 34.—Chieh Yü 婕妤, first century B.C. She was a lady of the court, a favorite of the Emperor Ch'eng, 32–6 B.C., of the Han dynasty. Her family name was Pan 班, and Chieh Yü was a title conferred upon the imperial secondary wife most distinguished for literary ability.

Chien-chang 建章, name of a palace in K'ai-feng 開封, Honan, once the eastern capital of the Han dynasty, A.D. 25–220 (see note to poem No. 31).

Chao-yang 昭陽, name of another palace of the same period at the same place.

Poem No. 35.—Bamboo Grove Monastery 竹林寺 was in the Lu-shan Hills in Kiangsi (see note to poem No. 19).

Poem No. 36.—Ch'ü Yüan's Temple, 三閭廟 San Lü Miao, the memorial temple dedicated to Ch'ü Yüan 屈原 or 屈子, the royal clansman and patriot of the state of Ch'u (see note to poems Nos. 18 and 20).

Yüan 沅 and Siang 湘, the names of two rivers in the province of Hunan, flowing into the Tung-t'ing Lake (see note to poem No. 32).

Ch'ü Yüan 屈原 was a statesman of the state of Ch'u who drowned himself when his prince rejected his advice. This event took place on the fifth day of the fifth month. In commemoration of this day the Chinese up to the present have offered rice wrapped in bamboo leaves, casting it into the river as a sacrifice to his spirit. The rice is wrapped to insure that it reaches the spirit before the fishes get it. The commemoration is the origin of the Dragonboat Festival, supposed to be in search of Ch'ü Yüan's body. In the southern provinces those who man the boats are dressed in varicolored costumes, some rowing, some playing music or setting off firecrackers, the affair ending in a boat race among the rivals.

Ch'ü Yüan was the author of the *Li Sao* 離騷, a celebrated poem of irregular meter describing his grief, usually translated "Dissipation of Sorrow," "Falling into Trouble," etc.

Poem No. 37.—Yi River 易水 in Yi-chou 易州, north of Pao-ting 保定, in Chili, now called Ho-pei province 河北.

Prince Tan of Yen 燕丹 died 226 B.C., according to Giles. He was a hostage in Ch'in 秦, but escaped in 230 B.C. He plotted against Ch'in by employing such bold men as Ching K'o 荊軻 to kill the Prince of Ch'in. The plot was not successful, and Ching K'o was himself killed in Ch'in. To appease the infuriated state of Ch'in, Prince Tan was killed by his father (for Ch'in see notes to poems Nos. 12 and 14; for Yen see note to poem No. 18).

"Hero" 壯士, "man of valor," refers to Ching K'o.

The second line of this poem literally translated is "The hero's hair lifted his hat from his head." This is hyperbole. My rendering is according to the spirit and not the letter.

Poem No. 41.—Sze 泗 水, a river in Shantung province.

Poem No. 43.—This is one of the poems with a double significance. The "poet's eyes" also means a statesman's keen sight to pick out men of talent. The second line means "budding talent," like young willows just developing but not yet turned into deep green. The third line suggests that a statesman should not wait to recognize a man's ability until he has attained full success; the fourth line concludes that if he does so, any ordinary person can do the same thing.

Poem No. 45.—The wine is the famous *t'u-su* 屠 蘇 of the Sung dynasty, also written 酴 酥.

"Peach charms" 桃 符 are made of two boards of peachwood, nailed to each side of the front door, and on those boards are painted the images of two spirits, Shen Shu 神 荼 and Yü Lei 鬱 壘, deified brothers who have power over demons and evil spirits. In more pretentious houses the pictures are carved on the doors and painted, while in ordinary homes printed pictures of the two spirits are pasted on the doors. These printed pictures are renewed every New Year. Sometimes they are dispensed with, and only couplets written on red paper are used.

Poem No. 46.—Chien Chang 建 章, name of one of the palaces of the Sung dynasty in K'ai-feng, Honan province. This Chien Chang Palace is not the same Chien Chang referred to in poem No. 34.

T'ung Ming Tien 通 明 殿, a throne hall in the above-mentioned Chien Chang Palace, where the Sung emperors held court.

Poem No. 47.—San-lang 三 郎, "Number Three," in the second line, is the nickname or a derisive term for the Emperor Ming Huang whose reign was A.D. 713-42.

Chiu Ling 九 齡, or Chang Chiu-ling 張 九 齡, A.D. 673-740, was one of the prime ministers of the fore-mentioned emperor.

Han Hsiu 韓 休, eighth century A.D., was another minister. Both were straightforward and outspoken, but Ming Huang never took their advice seriously. Han Hsiu died about A.D. 740, aged sixty-seven.

Poem No. 48.—"The Immortal's palm" 仙 人 掌. The T'ang emperors had a hall called the Ch'ao Yüan Ko 朝 元 閣 (New-year Audience Hall), to which, on the first day of the New Year, the reigning emperor went to worship God or the Lord of Heaven. In front of this hall were two pillars of considerable height;

on the top of each was the image of an Immortal holding a jade bowl to receive the dews of heaven, which were supposed to contain the elixir of life.

Poem No. 49.—"Rites and Music" 禮 樂 三 千 means a three-thousand-word essay on "Rites and Music." 禮 *li* (pronounced *lee*) are laws, statutes, and ceremonial regulations; 樂 *yüeh*, music, which is always in evidence at state and religious functions. The Chinese believe that it has a refining and civilizing influence on man and society.

Poem No. 50.—"Roses" 酴 醾 *t'u-mi*, also written 荼 蘼 *t'u-mi*, a pale-yellow climbing rose. Again called 薔 蘼 *ch'iang-mi*, or 薔 薇 *ch'iang-wei*, a variety of the cinnamon rose. *T'u-mi* is also the name of a wine whose color is like that of this rose. The botanical name is *Rubus*, or *Rubus rosifolius* Sm. This is from the authority of Mr. Matsumura whose book on botany makes mention of this flower.

Poem No. 51.—Tung-wu 東 吳 was one of the three kingdoms which struggled for supremacy between A.D. 220 and 277. It consisted of the greater parts of the present provinces of Kiangsu, Anhui, Hupei, and Hunan. Tung-wu is not the ancient feudal state of Wu 吳, mentioned in poem No. 24.

Poem No. 53.—All Souls' Day, 清 明 *Ch'ing Ming*, which means "clear and bright weather." This is also one of the Chinese solar calendar dates which occurs on or about the fifth of April. Poor and rich alike go to the graves of their dead to offer mock money, food, and flowers as well as to make repairs. Whole clans go to their first ancestor's grave on this day, carrying with them materials for an elaborate feast, cakes, fruits, fireworks, whole roast pigs, making it a picnic day on a large and sumptuous scale. If the grave is at a considerable distance, the members of the clan go by junks or sedan chair, the expenses being defrayed by the clan funds, which are derived from rents collected from clan fields or other property or interest from clan money invested in business enterprises. This worship of the ancestral grave by a whole clan on a large scale is more of a custom in the south than in the north of China.

"Almond-Town" 杏 花 村 (lit. "Apricot Blossom Village") is not an actual place, but the poet has given it this name to suit the season when apricots are generally in bloom.

Poem No. 54.—"New-made light" 新 火. Three days before All Souls' Day, in the Han dynasty (poem No. 56), no fire was allowed to be lighted, everybody eating cold food. Only at sunset on All Souls' Day was new fire produced and food allowed to be cooked and candles lighted.

·129·

Poem No. 55.—O-hu Hills 鵝湖山, Geese Lake Hills in Ch'ien-shan district 鉛山縣, Kwang-hsin prefecture 廣信府, Kiangsi province. This locality is noted for its vast crops of rice, 稻粱肥.

Poem No. 56.—Fasting Day or Cold Food Festival 寒食 occurred three days before *Ch'ing Ming*, or All Souls' Day. This fasting day is also known as 禁烟節, "Smoke-forbidden Festival" (see note to poem No. 54). In the time of the Han dynasty, waxen candles were lighted at sunset in the palace from newly made fire and sent to the prominent members of the imperial clansmen by command of the emperor.

Poem No. 57.—"Liquor banners" or "wine flags," 酒旗. These were displayed in ancient times in front of shops where wine was sold. Such flags, signs, or banners are seen to this day.

Poem No. 58.—The first couplet alludes to the imperial patronage which Kao P'ing 高駢 enjoyed while Kao Ch'an, author of this poem, being in an obscure position, had to wait for favors.

Poem No. 60.—"Pointed clogs" 屐齒 are made of wood with two diagonal pieces below, one in front, one behind, thus: ┳┳. A strap is nailed across on the top to hold the foot just behind the toes. A side view of a clog would look something like this: ⟨══⟩. The southern Chinese still wear them in the rainy season. The northern Chinese are unacquainted with the clog. All classes wear them in Japan, which adopted this footgear from the ancient Chinese.

Poem No. 61.—Lan Ling wine 蘭陵美酒, made in the prefecture of Yen-chou 兗州, in Shantung 山東 province.

Poem No. 63.—*Liu shu* 柳絮, usually translated by "willow catkin," but incorrectly. The definition of 絮 is 花之棉柔而飄揚者曰絮如柳絮楊絮蘆絮, "*Shu* is that soft and fluffy part which flies in the air, such as that of the willow, poplar, water-rushes, etc." The catkin, according to Webster's Dictionary, is ament, which again is defined as inflorescence consisting of a close-bracted spike, usually deciduous when mature. I wrote to Dr. Leighton Stuart, of Yenching University, and he referred the subject to Dr. C. S. Wu, the head of the biological department of the same university. Dr. Wu's note gives an elaborate explanation, with illustrations, of the catkin and the hairlike or plumelike outgrowths of the seed coat, found in milkweed, poplar, cotton, and willow. His conclusion is, "Catkin indicates only the types of flowers in clusters. The soft and fluffy material is not a part of the flower, but a part of the seed. It is the hairlike or plumelike outgrowths of the seed and may also be called the plume of the seed. *Liu shu* 柳絮 should therefore be translated 'the plume of the willow seed.' '' Thus science has helped poetry.

In my translation of the term I have used "willow-seed plume" as well as "willow down," according to the exigency of the rhythm.

The willow-seed plume is mentioned in poems Nos. 63, 82, 84, 86, and poplar-seed plume in Poem No. 78.

Poem No. 64.—Hsüan-tu kwan 立 都 觀, a Taoist temple in Ch'ang-an 長 安, the ancient capital of the T'ang dynasty. It is the present Hsi-an 西 安, capital of Shen-si province.

Poem No. 65.—The priests who reared those peach trees, 種 桃 道 士; also meant for the high officials who had Liu Yü-hsi 劉 禹 錫 exiled. The trees were the new set put into power by those high officials to strengthen their own party. After their fall Liu came back to office.

Poem No. 66.—Ch'u-chou 滁 州, a prefecture in An-hui province 安 徽.

The second couplet has a double meaning. The third line also intends to express the idea that the time is opportune for men of talent to be employed; the fourth line means that though the time is favorable, yet without higher recognition and patronage he, the poet, must idly wait, like an unmanned boat swinging at a deserted ferry.

Poem No. 68.—Northern Hills 北 山 outside the Ch'i-lin Gate 麒 麟 門 of the city of Nanking (see note to poem No. 15).

Poem No. 69.—The lake is the Hsi Hu 西 湖, or West Lake in Hangchow 杭 州, Chekiang province.

Hangchow was the capital of the Southern Sung dynasty 南 宋, A.D. 1127–1279 (see note to poem No. 104 and attached table of dates of the Sung dynasty).

Poem No. 70.—In my earlier translation I followed the commentator Wang Hsiang 王 相, who explained 稚 子 to mean "bamboo sprouts." But later I found in the K'ang-hsi Dictionary under the character "bamboo" 竹 a passage quoted from 贊 寧 筍 志, a work on bamboo shoots by Tsan Ning, a Buddhist priest of the Sung dynasty, that "there is a rodent called 竹 鼠, bamboo rat, the size of a cat, its color resembling that of the bamboo. It is called the 竹 豚, bamboo pig, or bamboo badger, also called the 稚 子 *chi tzǔ*. This is the animal meant by 筍 根 稚 子 in Tu Fu's poem." The rat or badger is gray while

·131·

the marmot is grayish yellow, more resembling the color of the bamboo. The rat is not the size of a cat.

Evidently Wang Hsiang and subsequent commentators did not know that 稚子 is the specific name of a rodent.

On a closer study of the poem I agree with the authority quoted by K'ang-hsi. The third and fourth lines of the poem are balanced sentences. 笋根, "at the bamboo-root," is opposed to 沙上, "on the sand shoals"; 稚子, "the marmot," a quadruped, is opposed to 凫雛, "wild duckling," a bird; 無人見, "by no person seen," is opposed to 傍母眠, "beside mother sleep."

By accepting K'ang-hsi's authority, the couplet becomes clear, and we are enabled to bring out the scheme of the balanced construction to a nicety.

The objection to accepting Wang Hsiang's view is that the bamboo root and bamboo sprout are objects too much alike and border on tautology.

Poem No. 74.—Lo-yang 洛陽, one of the two capitals of the Northern Sung dynasty before the Mongol invasion; the other capital was K'ai-feng. Both cities are in Honan province (see note to poem No. 2 and attached table of dates of the Sung dynasty).

Poem No. 75.—*Chou Yi* 周易, the "Book of Changes," or the *Yi Ching* of the Chou dynasty (see note to poem No. 20).

Poem No. 78.—The hidden meaning of this poem is the satirization of those who seize every occasion to make a display of their natural talents, as hinted in the second line, while men of a more simple character and less endowed by nature, like the poplar-down and elm-seeds, only follow their own inclination, flying hither and thither, preferring liberty and freedom rather than to seek their own interests.

Poem No. 85.—Ch'u Chou Road 衢州道 is the high road in Ch'u-chou prefecture in western Chekiang province.

Poem No. 87.—*P'i-p'a* 枇杷, also called loquat in South China. It is the medlar, a yellow fruit, the best being the 白沙枇杷, a light-yellow kind, from Tung-t'ing Shan 洞庭山, district in the Suchow prefecture.

Poem No. 89.—"Roses" 薔薇 *ch'iang-wei* (see note to poem No. 50).

Poem No. 94.—Chu-chiao Bridge 朱雀橋, outside of the city of Nanking. It was a great thoroughfare in the Tsin dynasty, A.D. 256–419, but in the T'ang dynasty it had become dilapidated and almost overgrown with weeds.

·132·

Wang 王 and Hsieh 謝 were two powerful families in the Tsin 晉 dynasty whose members held high official positions. In their mansions innumerable swallows built their nests. So noticeable was the fact that the street in which their mansions were situated was called Swallow Street, Wu-yi-hsiang 烏衣巷 (lit. Black-coat Street). The whole poem laments the vicissitudes and ephemeral span of human greatness.

Poem No. 95.—An-hsi 安西, literally: "the territory west of Ch'ang-an," then the capital of China. It was the general name for all the countries to the northwest, 西域諸國總名. At present it is known as Eastern Turkestan, north of Tibet and south of the Balkash Lake. The T'ang dynasty had a governor-general of An-hsi 安西都護使, or high commissioner of An-hsi, who ruled over the whole territory which comprised Kucha 龜茲, in the north; Karashar 焉耆, in the east; Khotan 于闐, in the south; and Kashgar 蘇勒 or 疏勒, in the west. There was also An-pei 安北, territory to the north of Ch'ang-an and south of Lake Baikal. The governor-general who ruled this territory was called 安北都護使, "governor-general of An-pei," and resided at Kucha.

Wei Ch'eng 渭城, city of Wei, situated on the northern bank of the Wei River and just west of Ch'ang-an.

Yang-kuan Pass 陽關, in the province of Kan-su 甘肅, to the southwest of Tun-huang district 敦煌縣, distance 130 *li* or about 40 English miles. It was the one pass through which all travelers had to go when journeying to the west.

Poem No. 96.—Ch'ang-sha 長沙, the present capital of Hunan province.

Ch'ang-an, the ancient name of the present city of Hsi-an 西安, in Shensi.

Yellow Crane Tower 黃鶴樓 was situated on the south bank of the Yangtze River and close to the city of Wu-ch'ang 武昌, opposite Hankow 漢口. It was burned and replaced about thirty years ago by an ugly building of foreign style, which does not harmonize with the surroundings or uphold the traditions connected with the tower.

Hsieh 榭 is a terrace on which buildings are erected, usually pavilions, consisting of a decorated roof supported by four pillars and without walls, thus giving the structures a light and airy appearance.

The 北榭碑 was the tablet under the roof of the pavilion on the northern terrace. There were four terraces in all.

Chiang ch'eng 江城, or "city by the river" refers to Wu-ch'ang 武昌.

·133·

The Round Tower 團城 in Peking is a *hsieh* 榭. It is between Coal Hill and the Marble Bridge. On it are erected a pavilion and some substantial buildings, including the temple in which the Jade Buddha is housed.

Poem No. 97.—Hwai Nan 淮南, the territory south of the Hwai River and north of the Yangtze River, extending from Hu-pei province in the west to Kiangsu province in the east (see note to poem No. 3).

Poem No. 99.—Ch'ih Hsi 七夕, the evening of the seventh day of the seventh month, is distinctly a maidens' festival in China. Long before the arrival of that evening, maidens gather to make beautiful little houses, temples, pagodas, tables, chairs, flower-designs, and various offerings, according to their notion and fancy. Such things are made of sesame seeds, flower seeds, or watermelon seeds, strung together with fine silk threads. The buds of the jasmine flower are also used. Artificial flowers are made of the pith of a plant, *Aralia papyrifera*, or pith of any kind. Miniature teasets, cups, plates, and dishes are made. Each maiden tries to show her special skill and design. When the particular evening has arrived the maidens come together to arrange all their work. Little temples and houses are placed in order. Tables and chairs are put in position. On the little tables are spread dishes of sweet meat, flowers in beautiful vases, everything giving the air of a sumptuous and elaborate feast. Only two pairs of silver chopsticks, two bowls, two plates, two winecups, are provided because it is a banquet offered only to the "weaver" 織女, Vega in Lyra, and "herdboy" 牛郎, Altair in Aquila, the two lovers of heaven, who are allowed to meet but once every year; the rest of the time they are separated by the Milky Way 天河, or the River of Heaven. On the evening of the seventh day of the seventh month, about midnight, these two stars can be seen overhead—in August, according to the Gregorian calendar.

Poem No. 100.—*Wu-t'ung* leaves 梧桐葉, the leaf of the Dryandra tree. The tree has smooth green bark and rather large leaves. The falling of its leaf is believed by the Chinese to be the first sign of coming autumn.

Poem No. 101.—Ch'ien niu Chih nü 牽牛織女, the "herdboy" and "weaver" (see note to poem No. 99).

Yin chu 銀燭, "silver candle," a poetic name for the moon.

Poem No. 102.—Milky Way 銀漢, the Silver Han River. Same as the River of Heaven 天河.

Yü p'an 玉 盤, "plate or tray of jade," is a poetic name for the full harvest moon. "The Milky Way is mute," as found in the Chinese text, has somewhat the meaning of "not being in evidence," or "invisible," because the moon is so extremely bright.

Poem No. 104.—Hsi Hu 西 湖, or West Lake, near Hangchow. This city of Hangchow was the capital of the Southern Sung dynasty 南 宋, A.D. 1127–1279, when the Chinese were driven by the Mongols to the south of the Yangtze River.

The two northern capitals were Lo-yang and Pien chou 汴 州, or Pien-liang, 汴 梁, in Honan province.

The last line of the poem, 直 把 杭 州 作 汴 州, "taking Hangchow for Pien-chou," might be aptly illustrated at present by saying that Nanking has taken the place of Peking since the removal of the capital to the south in 1928.

The West Lake is also mentioned in poem No. 69.

Poem No. 106.—Hsi Hu, West Lake (see notes to poems Nos. 69 and 111).

Hsi-tzǔ 西 子, or Hsi Shih 西 施, one of the most famous Chinese beauties, fifth century B.C.

Poem No. 107.—Yü-t'ang 玉 堂, Jade Hall, the Han-lin Academy 翰 林 院.

Poem No. 110.—This is a didactic poem, its hidden or double meaning being that those who wish to acquire true wisdom or a pure moral character must seek it from the very source or fountainhead.

Poem No. 111.—This is also a didactic poem. When it is not the proper time to undertake a work, you may tug and fret but no headway is gained. When the proper time comes, the work proceeds as if by itself, naturally and smoothly, without one's moving a finger. It illustrates the English adage, "Haste makes waste," and advocates patience and watchfulness.

It may be observed that both poems are from Chu Hsi 朱 熹, the great commentator of the Confucian classics and a great moral teacher.

Poem No. 112.—Hsi Hu, West Lake (see notes to poems Nos. 69, 104, 106). This poem has a deep and significant meaning beneath the mere wording. The brook is compared to an innocent character, uncontaminated by contact with the world. Whatever treatment it gets in its natural environment, whether good or bad, it takes as a matter of course. But once the water of the brook becomes part of the West Lake, helping to buoy up the barges of song and dance and all the frivolities of fashionable society, its original purity is gone forever.

·155·

Looking back to the days spent in the mountains, it will feel that much has been lost by the change.

Whenever I read this poem I always think of Robert Burns. When he was in his Highlands he was like his daisy growing in the Scottish fields—simple and natural. When he moved to London he was like a daisy transplanted into a hothouse. He was out of his natural environment and did not compare favorably with the highly cultivated plants of a great metropolis.

Poem No. 114.—Feng Ch'iao 楓橋, Maple Bridge, just outside of the city of Suchow.

The Han Shan Temple 寒山寺 is not far from the Maple Bridge. The temple was in ruins for a long time but rebuilt about 1900, the new buildings being rather poor structures. The famous bell was no more.

In the summer of 1911 I visited the place but it was altogether a disappointing sight. So was the visit to the Yellow Crane Tower in the same year.

Poem No. 116.—Ch'ing Nü 青女, the Young or Tender Maiden, is the goddess who presides over the frost; Su O 素娥, the Chaste or Fair Lady, is the fairy who reigns in the moon—also known as Ch'ang O.

Poem No. 117.—Lin Ho-ching 林和靖, whose personal name was Pu, was a poet and recluse of the Sung dynasty. He lived on a hill, the Mei Ling 梅嶺 in the Ku Shan Range 孤山, near the West Lake, spending his time in cultivating plum-flowers and keeping cranes. It was said of him that the plum-flower was his wife and the cranes his children.

The Chinese commentator states that he lived in seclusion in the latter part of the reign of Shen Tsung 神宗, A.D. 1068–78. Professor Giles puts down the dates of his life as A.D. 965–1026.

Poem No. 121.—Chung Jo-weng 鐘弱翁 was a dishonest and avaricious official of the Sung dynasty. The writer of this poem satirizes Chung by condemning riches and pomp, contented with plain face and pure conscience. Instead of revealing his real name, he signs himself "Cowherd."

Poem No. 122.—Ch'in-hwai 秦淮, a small stream outside the city wall of Nanking.

Shang nü 商女, "song-girls" or "singing-girls."

Hou T'ing Hua 後庭花, or "Flowers of the Back Garden," a sad song composed by 陳後主, the last prince of the principality of Ch'en, which was finally absorbed by the Sui 隋 dynasty (see notes to poem No. 19).

INDEX TO POETS

A

Ancient Hermit, poem No. 39

C

Chang Chi, T'ang, 8th cent. A.D., poem No. 114

Chang Yen, T'ang, poem No. 55

Chang Yüeh, T'ang, A.D. 667–730, poem No. 28

Chao Chia, Sung, 9th cent. A.D., poem No. 103

Chao Wu-chiu, Sung, A.D. 1053–1110, poem No. 47

Ch'en Tzŭ-ang, T'ang, A.D. 656–98, poem No. 31

Cheng Hao, Sung, A.D. 1032–85, poems Nos. 40, 97, 98

Cheng Ku, T'ang, 9th cent. A.D., poem No. 50

Chia Tao, T'ang, A.D. 777–841, poems Nos. 26, 81.

Chien Chi, T'ang, 8th cent. A.D., poems Nos. 18, 19

Chih Nan, T'ang, a Buddhist priest, poem No. 59

Ch'iu Wei, T'ang, poem No. 9.

Chou Pi-ta, Sung, 12th cent. A.D., poem No. 107.

Chu Fang, T'ang, 7th cent. A.D., poem No. 35

Chu Hsi, Sung, A.D. 1130–1200, poems Nos. 41, 92, 110, 111

Ch'u Kwang-hsi, T'ang, 8th cent. A.D., poem No. 4

Chu Shu-cheng, T'ang, 9th cent. A.D., poetess, poem No. 86

Chung Jo-weng, Sung, poem No. 121

E

Emperor Wen Tsung, T'ang, reigned A.D. 827–41, poem No. 25

F

Fan Ch'eng-ta, Sung, A.D. 1126–93, poems Nos. 90, 91

H

Han Hung, T'ang, 8th cent. A.D., poem No. 56

Han Yü, T'ang, A.D. 768–824, poems Nos. 44, 78

Herdboy, poem No. 121

Hermit, poem No. 39

Ho Chih-chang, T'ang, 7th and 8th cent. A.D., poem No. 11

Hsieh Fang-te, Sung, A.D. 1226–89, poems Nos. 77

Hsieh Yung, T'ang, poem No. 24

Hsü Yüan-chieh, Sung, poem No. 69

Huang-fu Jan, T'ang, poem No. 34

Hung Tsun, Sung, A.D. 1120–74, poem
No. 109

K

Kai Chia-yün, T'ang, poem No. 8

Kao Ch'an, T'ang, 9th cent. A.D.,
poem No. 58

Kao Pien, T'ang, 9th cent. A.D., poem
No. 89

Kao Shih, T'ang, 7th and 8th cent.
A.D., poem No. 16

Keng Wei, T'ang, 8th cent. A.D.,
poem No. 23

L

Li Po, T'ang, A.D. 705–62, poems Nos.
5, 29, 30, 61, 96

Li Shang-yin, T'ang, A.D. 813–58,
poem No. 116

Li She, T'ang, 9th cent. A.D., poem
No. 76

Li Shih-chih, T'ang, 8th cent. A.D.,
poem No. 17

Lin Ch'i, Sung, poems Nos. 48, 49,
104, 112

Ling-hu Ch'u, T'ang, 8th and 9th
cent. A.D., poem No. 10

Liu Chi-sun, Sung, poem No. 62

Liu K'o-chuang, Sung, 12th cent. A.D.,
poem No. 74

Liu Wu-tzǔ, Sung, poem No. 100

Liu Yü-hsi, T'ang, A.D. 772–842,
poems Nos. 21, 64, 65, 94

Lo Pin-wang, T'ang, 7th cent. A.D.,
poem No. 37

Lu Mei-po, Sung, poems Nos. 119, 120

M

Meng Hao-jan, T'ang, A.D. 689–740,
poems Nos. 1, 2, and 14

P

Pai Yü-ch'an, Sung, a priest, poem
No. 118

S

Ssǔ-k'ung Shu, T'ang, 8th cent. A.D.,
poem No. 38

Ssǔ-ma Kwang, Sung, A.D. 1019–86,
poems Nos. 82, 83

Su Shih, Sung, A.D. 1036–1101, poems
Nos. 42, 46, 52, 67, 105, 106, 113

Su T'ing, T'ang, A.D. 669–726, poem
No. 27

Sun Ti, T'ang, poem No. 7

T

Tai Fu-ku, Sung, 12th and 13th cent.
A.D., poem No. 87

Tai Shu-lun, T'ang, 9th cent. A.D.,
poem No. 36

Ts'ai Ch'io, Sung, 11th cent. A.D.,
poem No. 108

Ts'ao Pin, T'ang, poem No. 72

Ts'en Ts'an, T'ang, 8th cent. A.D.,
poem No. 33

Tseng Yü, Sung, 12th cent. A.D., poem
No. 85

Ts'ui Hao, T'ang, 8th cent. A.D.,
poem No. 15

Tu Fu, T'ang, A.D. 712–70, poems
Nos. 51, 63, 70

Tu Hsiao-shan, Sung, poem No. 115

Tu Mu, Sung, poems Nos. 53, 57, 101,
102, 122

W

Wang An-shih, Sung, A.D. 1021–86,
poems Nos. 45, 68, 88, 93

Wang Ch'ang-ling, T'ang, 8th cent.
A.D., poems Nos. 3, 32

Wang Ch'i, Sung, 11th cent. A.D.,
poems Nos. 73, 117
Wang Chia, T'ang, 9th and 10th cent.
A.D., poem No. 71
Wang Chih-huan, T'ang, poem No. 6
Wang Feng-yüan, Sung, 13th cent.
A.D., poem No. 80
Wang Wei, T'ang, A.D. 699–759, poems
Nos. 13, 95
Wang Yü-cheng, Sung, 10th cent.
A.D., poem No. 54
Wei Ying-wu, T'ang, 8th cent. A.D.,
poems Nos. 20, 22, 66

Y

Yang Chien, Sung, 12th and 13th cent.
A.D., poems Nos. 79, 84
Yang Ch'iung, T'ang, 7th cent. A.D.,
poem No. 12
Yang Chü-yüan, T'ang, 8th and 9th
cent. A.D., poem No. 43
Yang P'o, Sung, 10th cent. A.D., poem
No. 99
Yeh Li, Sung, poem No. 75
Yeh Shih, Sung, A.D. 1150–1223, poem
No. 60

CHRONOLOGICAL TABLES

T'ANG DYNASTY, A.D. 618–906

Dynastic Title	A.D.	Title of Reign
Kao Tsu	618	Wu Tê
T'ai Tsung	627	Chêng Kuan
Kao Tsung	650	Yung Hui
Chung Tsung	684	Ssǔ Shêng
Jui Tsung	684	Wên Ming
Wu Hou (empress, usurper)	684	Kuang Tsê
Chung Tsung (resumes throne)	705	Shên Lung
Jui Tsung	710	Ching Yün
Hsüan Tsung	713	K'ai Yüan
Su Tsung	756	Chih Tê
Tai Tsung	763	Kuang Tê
Tê Tsung	780	Chien Chung
Shun Tsung	805	Yung Chêng
Hsien Tsung	806	Yüan Ho
Mu Tsung	821	Ch'ang Ch'ing
Ching Tsung	825	Pao Li
Wên Tsung	827	T'ai Ho
Wu Tsung	841	Hui Ch'ang
Hsüan Tsung	847	T'ai Chung
I Tsung	860	Hsien T'ung
Hsi Tsung	874	Ch'ien Fu
Chao Tsung	889	Lung Chi
Chao Hsüan Ti	905	T'ien Yu

Capital: CH'ANG-AN, Shen-si province.

SUNG DYNASTY, A.D. 960–1279

Dynastic Title	A.D.	Title of Reign
T'ai Tsu	960	Chien Lung
T'ai Tsung	976	T'ai P'ing
Chên Tsung	998	Hsien P'ing
Jên Tsung	1023	T'ien Sheng
Ying Tsung	1064	Chih P'ing
Shên Tsung	1068	Hsi Ning
Chê Tsung	1086	Yüan Yu
Hui Tsung	1101	Chien Chung
Ch'in Tsung	1126	Ching K'ang

The foregoing is known as the Northern Sung, before the Mongol invasion. Capital: PIEN-CHOU, Honan province.

Dynastic Title	A.D.	Title of Reign
Kao Tsung	1127	Chien Yen
Hsiao Tsung	1163	Lung Hsing
Kuang Tsung	1190	Shao Hsi
Ning Tsung	1195	Ch'ing Yüan
Li Tsung	1225	Pao Ch'ing
Tu Tsung	1265	Hsien Shun
Kung Tsung	1275	Tê Yu
Tuan Tsung	1276	Ching Yen
Ti Ping	1278	Hsiang Hsing

The foregoing is known as the Southern Sung, driven by the Mongols to the south. Capital: HANGCHOW, Chekiang province.

POPES AND BISHOPS OF ROME, A.D. 590–1281

Pontiff	Pontificate A.D.	Nationality
Gregory I, the Great	590–604	Roman
Sabinianus	604–606	Tuscan
Boniface III	607	Roman
Boniface IV	608–615	From Abruzzi
Deusdedit	615–618	
Boniface V	619–625	

Pontiff	Pontificate A.D.	Nationality
Honorius	625–638	From Capua
Severinus	638–640	Roman
John IV	640–642	From Dalmatia
Theodore	642–649	Greek
Martin I	649–653	From Tudertum
Eugenius I	654–657	Roman
Vitalianus	657–672	From Signia
Adeodatus	672–676	Roman
Donus I	676–678	Roman
Agatho	678–681	Sicilian
Leo II	682–683	....
Benedict II	684–685	Roman
John V	685–686	From Syria
Conon	686–687	From Thrace
Sergius	687–701	From Palermo
John VI	701–705	Greek
John VII	705–707	Greek
Sisinnius	708	Syrian
Constantinus I	708–715	....
Gregory II	715–731	Roman
Gregory III	731–741	Syrian
Zachary	741–752	Greek
Stephen II	752–757	....
Paul I	757–767	Roman
Stephen III	768–772	Sicilian
Adrian I	772–795	Roman
Leo III	795–816	Roman
Stephen IV	816–817	Roman
Pascal I	817–824	Roman
Eugenius II	824–827	Roman
Valentine	827	Roman
Gregory IV	827–844	Roman
Sergius II	844–847	Roman
Leo IV	847–855	Roman
Benedict	855–858	Roman

Pontiff	Pontificate A.D.	Nationality
Nicholas I	858–867	Roman
Adrian II	867–872	Roman
John VIII	872–882	Roman
Martin II	882–884	Roman
Adrian III	884–885	Roman
Stephen V	885–891	Roman
Formosus	891–896	Bishop of Parto
Boniface VI	896	. . . .
Stephen VI	896–897	Roman
Romanus	897	. . . .
Theodore II	897	. . . .
John IX	898–900	Native of Tiber
Benedict IV	900–903	Roman
Leo V	903	Native of Ardea
Sergius III	904–911	. . . .
Anastasius III	911–913	Roman
Landon	913–914	Native of Sabina
John X	914–929	Roman
Leo VI	929	Native of Rome
Stephen VII	929–931	Roman
John XI	931–936	. . . .
Leo VII	936–939	Roman
Stephen VIII	939–942	Roman
Martin III	942–946	. . . .
Agapetus II	946–955	. . . .
John XII	955–964	. . . .
Benedict V	965	Roman
John XIII	965–972	Roman
Benedict VI	973–974	. . . .
Benedict VII	974–983	Roman
John XIV	983–984	. . . .
John XV	985–996	Roman
Gregory V	996–999	. . . .
Sylvester II	999–1003	Native of Auvergne
John XVII	1003	. . . .

·143·

Pontiff	Pontificate A.D.	Nationality
John XVIII	1003–1009	Roman
Sergius IV	1009–1012	. . . .
Benedict VIII	1012–1024	Roman
John XIX	1024–1033	. . . .
Benedict IX	1033–1045	Tusculum
Gregory VI	1045–1046	Roman
Clement II	1046–1047	Saxony
Damascus II	1048	. . . .
Leo IX	1048–1054	Bishop of Toul
Victor II	1054–1057	Bishop of Eichstadt
Stephen IX	1057–1058	Abbot of Monte Cassino
Nicholas II	1058–1061	Native of Burgundy
Alexander II	1061–1073	Native of Milan
Gregory VII	1073–1085	Native of Tuscany
Victor III	1086–1087	Native of Beneventum
Urban II	1088–1099	French
Pascal	1099–1118	Native of Tuscany
Gelasius	1118–1119	Native of Gaeta
Calixtus II	1119–1124	Native of Burgundy
Honorius II	1124–1130	Bishop of Ostia
Innocent II	1130–1143	Roman
Celestine II	1143–1144	Tuscan
Lucius II	1144–1145	Bologna
Eugenius III	1145–1153	Native of Pisa
Agnastasius IV	1153–1154	Roman
Adrian IV	1154–1159	English
Alexander III	1159–1181	Native of Siena
Lucius III	1181–1185	Native of Lucca
Urban	1185–1187	Bishop of Milan
Gregory VIII	1187	Native of Beneventum
Clement III	1187–1191	Bishop of Praeneste
Celestine III	1191–1198	Roman
Innocent III	1198–1216	Native of Signia
Honorius III	1216–1227	Roman

Pontiff	Pontificate A.D.	Nationality
Gregory IX	1227–1241	Native of Anagni
Celestine IV	1241	Native of Milan
Innocent IV	1243–1254	Native of Genoa
Alexander IV	1254–1261	Native of Anagni
Urban IV	1261–1264	Frenchman
Clement IV	1265–1268	Native of St. Gilles-sur-Rhône
Gregory X	1271–1276	Native of Piacenza
Innocent V	1276	Native of Tarentaise
Adrian V	1276	Native of Genoa
John XXI	1276–1277	Native of Lisbon
Nicholas III	1277–1281	Roman

This table of the popes and bishops of Rome is prepared to supply the dates lacking in the table of the kings of England. These two combined will give the periods corresponding to the T'ang and Sung dynasties and help the reader to get the proper historical perspective.

This and the table of the kings of England are taken from Dr. Henry W. Ruoff's *Standard Dictionary of Facts* (ed. 1914), published by the Frontier Press Company of Buffalo, New York.

KINGS OF ENGLAND, A.D. 827–1399

ANGLO-SAXON LINE

Name	Reign A.D.	Birth A.D.	Death
Egbert	827–837	775?	837
Ethelwuff	838–857	....	858
Ethelbald	857–860	....	860?
Ethelbert	860–866	....	866?
Ethelred I	866–871	....	871
Alfred the Great	871–901	849	901
Edward the Elder	901–924	870?	924
Ethelatan	925–940	895?	941
Edmund I	940–946	923	946
Edred	946–955	....	955

Name	Reign A.D.	Birth A.D.	Death
Edwy	955–959	939?	959
Edgar	959–975	943?	975
Edward the Martyr	975–978	961?	978
Ethelred II	978–1016	....	1016
Edmund Ironside	1016–1017	989	1017

DANISH LINE

Name	Reign A.D.	Birth A.D.	Death
Canute	1017–1035	995	1035
Harold I (Harefoot)	1035–1040	....	1040
Hardicanute	1040–1042	1019	1042

SAXON LINE

Name	Reign A.D.	Birth A.D.	Death
Edward the Confessor	1041–1066	1004	1066
Harold II	1066	1022	1066

NORMAN LINE

Name	Reign A.D.	Birth A.D.	Death
William I	1066–1087	1027	1087
William II	1087–1100	1056	1100
Henry I	1100–1135	1068	1135
Stephen	1135–1154	1105	1154

PLANTAGENET LINE

Name	Reign A.D.	Birth A.D.	Death
Henry II	1154–1189	1133	1189
Richard I, the Lion-hearted	1189–1199	1157	1199
John	1199–1216	1166	1216
Henry III	1216–1272	1207	1272
Edward I	1272–1307	1239	1307
Edward II	1307–1327	1284	1327
Edward III	1327–1377	1312	1377
Richard II	1377–1399	1366	1399

The foregoing table is prepared to give readers of the Anglo-Saxon race a more accurate historical perspective of the contemporaneous periods of the T'ang and Sung dynasties and to enable such readers to know when their ancestors flourished at the time these Chinese poets sang their songs.

⟦ PRINTED IN U·S·A· ⟧

JUL 15 1942